Today's Christian Woman

ANN WARREN

D1741491

KINGSWAY PUBLICATIONS
EASTBOURNE

ISBN 0 86065 268 8

Scripture quotations are from The Living Bible,
copyright © Tyndale House Publishers 1971.

Cover photo: Tony Stone Photolibrary—London

KINGSWAY PUBLICATIONS LTD
Lottbridge Drove, Eastbourne, E. Sussex BN23 6NT
Typeset by Nuprint Services Ltd, Harpenden, Herts.
Printed and bound in Great Britain
by Collins, Glasgow

Contents

1. A Woman's Place

Confusion reigns in the life of today's woman. On the one hand she is being urged by Women's Lib to march bravely into the future declaring herself to be equal to or better than her male counterpart. And on the other hand the traditional loyalties of home and family tug away at her heart strings, making her wonder what kind of life she really needs or wants anyway. Meanwhile the world has clocked up its fourth woman Prime Minister, and any number of successful women in most sections of business life.

Thousands of men are out of work in a recession such as the world has never seen before. Some Christians are asking whether the women should not stand down and allow men to take up their jobs. But how essential is the traditional role of the man as breadwinner, and how central to our Christian beliefs? If, for example, a woman can get a job when her husband is out of work, or go out to work to help ends meet, isn't it only right that she should do so?

Magazine and newspaper articles are constantly telling us that we need bigger and better things to make us happy, but how much is enough? And while a mother may feel she needs the stimulation of an interesting career, isn't the security of her presence in the family more important than anything else? The fact that a married woman may now be able to choose whether or not to take up paid employment brings its own built-in tensions along with the opportunities. How is she to come to the right decisions on all these crucial issues?

Those of us who look for guidance to the church have not always found help here. Some Christians have rushed to find an answer to the problems presented by 'equal opportunities' and come up with an 'instant solution' in the doctrine of 'submission', together with the insistence that a woman's place is in the home and at the kitchen sink.

But ironically the many married women who struggle with housework and caring for small children are often made to feel that what they do is of little intrinsic value in a world that lays all its emphasis on academic achievement and financial reward. Journalists in popular magazines have struggled over the years to dream up a wage packet for this very full time career of housekeeper and nanny, shopper and chauffeur all rolled into one, but it remains a problem that the housewife herself often feels that she achieves very little that is worthwhile.

For many of us who lead normal secular lives looking after our families and going about our everyday work, the issue of 'equality' may not seem to be of any great significance. But every so often its shadow falls across our lives, making us wake up with a jolt to question what our status really is. Are women really some kind of inferior creation put on this earth simply to serve their menfolk? Or doesn't Genesis teach that we are different from men, but at the same time equal before God?

The wife of a well-known evangelical living overseas was quite shattered recently by the negative response she received at a large student gathering where she had been asked to speak while home on leave. The reaction had nothing whatever to do with the content of her talk, which everyone agreed was excellent, but simply to the fact that as a mere woman they obviously felt that she should never have been asked to speak in the first place.

Doctrinally sound as some Christians may feel this to be, it is not an attitude calculated to bring out the best in anyone, and it is certainly not love. Women respond to love and encouragement, and it is this which enables them to be themselves and to use their gifts more effectively. Unloving male domination has produced nothing but aggressive feminism.

When Jesus walked this earth two thousand years ago, He spoke to and encouraged many different women, often seriously upsetting the disciples who found his attitude hard to cope with! In those days women were regarded as chattels to possess and were seldom even educated. So the fact that he spent so much time talking with them, and entrusting much of his valuable teaching to them was little short of revolutionary.

Since Jesus offered so much encouragement to women that acceptance of them became one of the hallmarks of New Testament Christianity, one might well have expected the church to be in the forefront of the campaign for women's rights today. Instead, however, we hear a great deal more about the letters of Paul, who is rapidly (if unjustifiably!) becoming the patron saint of all male chauvinists.

In some churches today the three negative Pauline passages on the subject of women have been so minutely examined under a microscope—and some might say well magnified in the process—that much of the other scriptural teaching about women has been bypassed. For example we often hear about women not being permitted to teach, and about the natural headship of men, but nobody mentions the fact that Romans 16 indicates that ten women and nineteen men were actually involved in the ministry of the Roman church; or that the church in Philippi began with a prayer meeting in the house of the businesswoman, Lydia. Then there is Phoebe, who clearly occupied the official role of a deacon, although that word was often translated as 'helper' by male translators, who obviously couldn't cope with the implications of the original! Whatever the negative and apparently prohibitive verses about women imply—and there are a number of possible interpretations, which we will come to in a later chapter—it is clear that women did share in the ministry of the early church and that Jesus Himself greatly valued the women He knew.

Realizing this, and feeling the call of God to either full or part-time ministry, some of today's Christian women are confused and hurt by what they see as the church's rejection of them. In some denominations they will not be allowed to progress beyond the bottom rung of the ecclesiastical ladder, while their male colleagues, with whom they trained at theological college, mount above them. In the meantime, many of the house churches are rushing backwards into an insistence on the subordination of women, even instructing that their heads should be covered at all times!

Of course we must realize the vital importance of giving our homes and families top priority in our lives. With so many broken homes, so many needy children and so much unhappiness, the natural loving, caring and home-making gifts of womankind are at an all-time premium. But this positive approach should replace the counter-productive 'put her in her place' submission we hear so much about. In Proverbs 31 you will not find a patronizing pat on the back for the 'little woman' at home with the washing machine and the gentle sudsy soap. Instead there is an enthusiastic round of applause for the woman whose influence on her husband, her children and the business world around her, was such that the writer ends 'give her credit for all she does, because she deserves the respect of everyone'.

We also have to see what this chauvinistic attitude does to women who are not married or whose gifts are clearly intended for use outside the home. It is less than helpful to speak of women only as homemakers or mother figures. This implies that all other women are inadequate or are merely living out God's second-best for their lives, which is surely equivalent to telling God that He got it wrong when He made them! The truth is that the time available to the single woman (or the married woman with older children) can be greatly used in the service of God in a hundred different ways.

Changes taking place today

For so many centuries it has been asserted that a woman's place is in the home, that any change in this attitude was almost guaranteed to cause alarm and despondency. After all it was only comparatively recently that women were even allowed the vote, and more recently still that they were admitted to certain august bodies like the Stock Exchange. So it was almost a foregone conclusion that those of us struggling to rethink Christian attitudes to women at the close of the twentieth century should be caught up in the vortex of a storm. But what are the rights and wrongs for Christian women today, and how do we face up to them?

If I had to use one word that expressed all that I feel to be wrong with our understanding of a woman's role in society, it would be the word 'narrow'. Instead of looking at our God-given femininity and asking what He would have us do with this in today's world, we have tried only to look backwards and to take as our ideal what was done in the past.

But tradition is not, and never has been, a reliable guide. For example, one reason that women have for so long spent their time in and around the home was simply that running a house was an all consuming career. Without running water, machines, gas and electricity, the ordinary household chores took up the whole working day so completely that at the end there was little energy left for anything else.

However, although the work was time-consuming and hard, it was I believe much more varied than the average housewife's work today. This was certainly true of the ideal woman pictured in Proverbs Chapter 31. This lady, who was King Lemuel's 'ideal', was quite a business woman in her own right, managing her own sizeable household, buying imported food from the merchants, planting out a vineyard in a field she had bought herself. She was also very creative, making her own clothes and spinning cloth; moreover she always had time to help people in need around her. The life of the average suburban housewife seems very narrow in comparison.

Before the industrial revolution, the country wife had more in common with the housewife in Proverbs, than does today's housewife. Probably she ran her own smallholding with chickens, a pig and even a cow or goat. She also often had her own cottage industry, spinning wool or flax. If she worked as a servant in a large household she at least mixed with a great many other people.

But as the cottage industries were swallowed up by the factories of the industrial revolution and large households were eventually replaced by small suburban villas which could be run by one woman with a minimum of help, so the role of the ordinary housewife has dwindled to the supermarket and the washing machine. We need the home base for rearing children, but the woman herself has lost the sense of value engendered by managing her own smallholding or cottage industry or working in a large household. Incidentally, it was not until the industrial revolution that the husband came to be regarded as the sole breadwinner—this was a Victorian and not necessarily Christian ideal at all!

Much of the frustration experienced by women today is caused by the narrowness of lifestyle imposed upon her. Houses are generally getting smaller and duller, and families are having to move away from relatives and friends to enormous, faceless housing estates which have no sense of belonging.

Clearly a Christian wife and mother must make it a priority to create a home for her family, but is this all that her life is to consist of? And why have Christians regarded the Victorian picture of the ideal woman as the only model possible?

Denying God's gifts

The real problem is that all the controversy about a 'woman's place' seems to be trapping us into preconceived roles, rather than recognizing the individuality which has been given us by God.

Personally I hate even putting the word 'housewife' as my occupation on a form, because in that single word I feel as if I lose my God-given identity and become just another household statistic. If the word were wife, or mother, or even homemaker, then somehow it would not feel nearly so restrictive. There is something about the word 'housewife' that expresses all that I feel about the traditionally narrow role that seems to have been handed down to us. Or, as a friend of mine said the other day, I did not marry the house, I married my husband! The word implies that married women have automatically become housekeepers and nothing more.

God did not mass-produce female shapes who would all fulfil the same role. He made individual women who would each separately hear His voice and follow Him. Many women marry and have children, and are content to centre their lives entirely on the home. But it does not follow that this must be the only blueprint for a woman's role. Not only is that patently absurd, it is also a denial of the individuality that Christians believe God has given to each one of us.

The problem with feminism

Some campaigners for Women's Liberation have done a great deal of harm to many ordinary women quietly trying to find a bit more freedom in their lives. The angry bitter attitudes shown by some feminists has, I believe, alienated many otherwise sympathetic people. It has also meant that virtually any woman working outside the home, or speaking up for what she believes, is liable to be branded with this label—and with attitudes that she may well not whole-heartedly subscribe to.

Another unfortunate by-product of feminism is the way in which a younger generation has gained the impression that they can simultaneously have a successful career and a happy marriage and children, without losing out in any way. A recent magazine article by a well-known feminist admitted that while listening to her own daughter and other women of that generation, she had seen something 'out of focus' and badly wrong in the way that they were trying to live out the 'equality' that she and others had fought so hard to gain. The implication that they could be 'superwomen' running a home and family with one hand, and holding down a stimulating demanding career with the other, was simply not working out in practice.

Effectively the woman at home may now feel guilty because she is not out earning her share, while the woman at work feels she ought to be able to cope running her home and family as before.

The Christian must be guided only by biblical values and priorities, but it seems to me that the church has often failed us by not helping us to see how these apply in today's world. The panic cry for a return to the 'good old days' when women were safely tucked away at the kitchen sink is not an answer but a retreat! We must listen not to the voice of human tradition or past culture, or to instructions born out of fear, but to what the Holy Spirit is saying to us today.

2. Women God Chose

What went wrong?

In Genesis the man and woman were equal before God. Since Jesus Himself gave to the women in His life an affirmation and acceptance that was quite revolutionary and since this continued in the first century church, it has always been a complete mystery to me how and why it did not remain one of the hallmarks of Christianity down the ages.

Viewed in the light of the twentieth century, the early involvement of women in the life of the early church does not seem particularly unusual but in first century Israel it was amazing. At that time women were thought to be totally inferior and a dangerous temptation to men, to be hidden away safely at home and ignored. Women were not permitted to worship with their menfolk in the Synagogues but were segregated behind a screen. They could be divorced at will by their husbands, who only had to hand them a note of dismissal, yet a woman could not divorce her husband. Furthermore, no woman was ever permitted to act as a witness, which makes Jesus' choice of women as witnesses to the most momentous event of all time on Easter Sunday all the more remarkable!

Although some more cynical men have asked why Jesus did not choose a female disciple if he valued women so much, the really unusual thing for those days was that He did choose a great many women to serve Him, allowing them to travel round with Him, as Luke chapter 18 records. So what put a stop to this progress?

Patricia Gundry in her book *Heirs Together* says the blame should be laid at the door of the Gnostics, second-century heretical groups who believed, amongst other things, that the physical body was intrinsically evil, and that all its desires should be suppressed. Denial of the physical body therefore became a way for the faithful to gain spiritual merit. Since the sexual desires of mankind were an obvious example of this 'evil', it was a logical step to say that the object of those desires—woman—must herself be evil. Woman was such a temptation to man that her new-found freedom had to be curtailed. The church returned once more to the negative attitude towards womankind that had prevailed before Christ brought us the good news of our freedom.

God's ideal for women

Of course it is true that a woman is physically weaker and more vulnerable than her counterpart, and needs Christian headship and protection. Our emotional make-up alone puts us more at risk. A combination of our vulnerability in child-bearing and the hormonal swings that occur at different times of the month can make our emotions quite difficult to handle at times. Women whether at home or at work, are generally more easily hurt by difficult situations and angry words, and are less able to cope with the cut and thrust of life. We were made as complementary individuals to men and we need their strength, their objectivity and their protection at difficult times.

But equally, our very sensitivity and vulnerability makes us more ready to recognize our need of God and of His daily power and protection. While a man is often too busy to acknowledge his need of a Saviour, a woman knows her need because it is an integral part of her own make-up. I believe it is no accident that there are often so many more women in church than men.

To do justice to the subject, a study of the many different women in the Bible and the reasons why God chose and used them as He did, should take a whole book but a few instances will give us some useful pointers to God's blueprint for womankind.

A woman fully committed to God

Mary, the mother of Jesus, has been venerated by the church for centuries both as the perfect symbol of womankind and as the ideal, stay-at-home wife and mother. Ironically, with the possible exception of the annunciation, the Bible narrative *never* shows Mary at home—we see her for example, at Bethlehem for the census, going up to Jerusalem for the Passover, and at Cana for the wedding.

Surely Mary was chosen because she loved God with her whole heart and was ready to submit to the plan He had for her life, whatever that might involve. Certainly to be chosen to give birth to the Son of God Himself was the most tremendous honour possible, but perhaps we too readily overlook the cost to Mary.

Imagine explaining to your fiancé, in an age where women were stoned for adultery and publicly disgraced for the slightest misdemeanour, that you are only pregnant because the Holy Spirit has come upon you! In actual fact, until the child was born and the shepherds and the kings came to confirm what the angel had promised, Mary had to trust God's word alone. It was on God's promise about Jesus that she staked everything in her life that she held dear—her fiancé, her reputation, her whole future. Here was a young girl who truly trusted God with everything she had and held nothing back.

In today's practical and materialistic society many of us have problems trusting God with even the smallest aspects of our lives and as a result we so often miss out on the wonderful things He has in store for us. To quote D. L. Moody—'The world has yet to see what God can do with a man (or woman!) who is wholly committed to Him!'

Should a woman ever take the lead?

Deborah, the prophetess in Judges, is definitely a woman we should look at in today's world.

Israel's leader at that time, the one who was responsible for bringing the people back to God, was Deborah, a prophetess, the wife of Lappidoth. She held court at a place now called Deborah's Palm Tree, between Ramah and Bethel, in the hill country of Ephraim; and the Israelites came to her to decide their disputes.

One day she summoned Barak, son of Abinoam, who lived in Kedesh, in the land of Naphthali, and said to him, 'The Lord God of Israel has commanded you to mobilize ten thousand men from the tribes of Naphthali and Zebulun. Lead them to Mount Tabor to fight

King Jabin's mighty army with all his chariots, under General Sisera's command. The Lord says, "I will draw them to the Kishon river, and you will defeat them there."'

'I will go, but only if you go with me!' Barak told her.

'All right,' she replied, 'I will go with you; but I am warning you now that the honour of conquering Sisera will go to a woman instead of you.' So she went with him to Kedesh (Judges 4:4–9).

Some Christian men today are saying that if only the women would keep silent and take a back seat again, then the men would automatically take up their rightful position of leadership—in other words, it is the women who are preventing them from doing this! I wonder! Certainly, many women prefer to encourage and help their menfolk rather than take the lead themselves. But what if, like Deborah, God is calling them to take action, to re-awake the nation to what he is saying? Did Deborah just sit under her palm tree, saying and doing nothing, just hoping that Barak and the others would wake up and hear God too?

It seems to me that Deborah's action was a very fair one. When Barak asked her to go with him, she accepted, but warned him of the consequences—that the glory would go to a woman. She had done her best, she had found and encouraged the necessary man to take action, but she did not hold back from going along too if it was really necessary.

If God points out to us something that needs doing we should first look for, and encourage, a man to head this up. But if there is no one, then surely we are not supposed to sit and do nothing? Deborah should be an inspiration to all of us. Indeed, a Roman Catholic friend of mine is very fond of saying, 'At times of crisis a woman has always appeared to save the day!'

Don't be afraid to use your gifts

There are more copies of the book of Esther in existence in Israel than any other Old Testament documents. Yet Esther is not nearly so well-known in the West—which is strange, as there are a number of parallels between Esther and today's Christian woman.

This young Jewish girl, Esther, was chosen to be Queen of the vast empire of the Medes and the Persians, through nothing more than a beauty competition! She found herself married to a tyrant king, Xerxes, just at the time when a decree was being sent out to all corners of this vast empire ordering a wholesale massacre of Jewish men, women and children. Her uncle Mordecai pointed out that God must have put her where she was for a purpose and pushed her to do something quickly. The rest of the story can be found in the tense, action-packed chapters of Esther, sandwiched between Nehemiah and the book of Job. What matters here is how Esther went about her task.

Despite her very understandable fear of the tyrant king, who had been known to execute people simply for coming into his presence without being summoned, she found herself forced to take action. First she and her friends fasted and prayed and then she waited for God to show her what to do. Humanly speaking, Esther's greatest assets were her beauty and her position as Queen—and she used both to the full.

So often Christian women almost apologize for

their very existence, as if ashamed of the beauty God has given them. But an attractive, well-dressed Christian woman will make a greater impact on the world outside than one who is creeping around in dowdy clothes, refusing to make the best of herself. Whether we like it or not, people judge our God by the calibre of his followers—and so often we play down the gifts that God has given us!

Christians also must not be afraid to accept positions of power and influence in the world of politics, business, sport or the arts because they may witness for God in those areas. Today we are reaping the harvest of a generation of Christians who believed that to have anything to do with the media was somehow inherently sinful. The result? A gaping hole because people who had positions of influence left to get involved in more Christian work or never dared to enter this world in the first place! Wherever you may find yourself may be exactly the place where God plans to use you, so stay with it, just as Esther did, unless you get very clear instructions to the contrary.

Care of the old

The story of Ruth must be a favourite of many reading this book. After the death of her husband, when it would have been so much easier to turn to her own people and look after her own interests, she refused to leave her mother-in-law to cope alone, but went with her into a strange land saying, 'Your people shall be my people, and your God, my God.'

Self-interest and personal fulfilment are so integral a part of life in the world around us that Ruth's actions seem strangely out of place today. Old people

live and die alone or are tucked away in some retire-
ment home and all the emphasis is placed on the
young ones being free to lead their own lives
unfettered. Loneliness and a terrible sense of being
unwanted affects a huge and ever-growing section of
the community, as our old folk live longer and longer.

Although it may not be desirable or possible to
have elderly parents living with us, they need to see
us and know we care about them and want them.
They need to feel that they are of real value to us.

The old person that God is asking us to care for
may well not be a part of our own family—perhaps
someone in the neighbourhood with no family or
friends nearby or just an old man that God particularly lays on our hearts. But just as Ruth's action led
her to become the great-grandmother of King David,
so the blessings that God brings to those who care for
these old people will be much greater than any of us
ever realize at the time.

Today's Christian woman

Although her blueprint was written down hundreds
of years before Christ, the picture of the ideal woman
portrayed in Proverbs chapter 31 must surely be the
most relevant and the most up-to-date for married
women trying to lead Christian lives at the close of
the twentieth century. This truly good wife fulfils the
domestic and supportive duties of a wife and mother
and still realizes to the full the opportunities that
surround her in the world outside. It would have
been easy for her to say that all her time and her
energy were taken up with running this large household, bringing in food from the merchants and pre-
paring meals for everyone, but she does not! Rising

before dawn, and working far into the night, she is an energetic and a hard worker, actually looking for opportunities and needs she can meet in the world around her. To be fair, the amount this lady achieves is made possible by a household of servants, but what is important is what she does with her time and her lack of laziness.

Many women who do not have to go out to work today seem to lack any kind of vision about what they can usefully do with their time. Perhaps their husbands do not want them to go out to work or they lack the necessary training, but then surely there is all the more reason to become wholeheartedly involved in the opportunities for service that surround them! The poor and the needy are still in evidence today, despite the provisions of the welfare state, whilst the lonely and elderly are more in need of help than they have ever been. As whole village communities have been split up and families dispersed around the globe in search of work, so we have become more insular and self-protective in our thinking, with everything centring on our own little families tucked away safely behind our own front doors.

I believe that the church itself has been far too inward looking. It may encourage the womenfolk to attend the Bible study or get involved with church activities, but what policy does the church have about the many hundreds of needs and opportunities in the community? The Christian woman could be salt and light in the community. If she were governed by wisdom and kindness she could be a very badly needed signpost to God in the hospital or the supermarket, in the office or the factory.

Women Jesus met

Jesus befriended so many women that it would be difficult to single out just one or two for comment. He spoke to them, taught them, healed them and rescued them and entrusted to them some of the most remarkable contents of His life's teaching. It was, for example, to the despised Samaritan woman that He first revealed the fact that He was the Messiah and to Martha of Bethany that He spoke those lovely words, so well-known from the funeral service, 'I am the resurrection and the life.' More incredible still, He entrusted women with the responsibility of first witnessing to His resurrection on Easter Sunday.

Since Jesus accepted men and women equally with such loving and open generosity it is sad to see how often male commentators have twisted and altered the stories. Dorothy Pape, in her book *God's Ideal Woman* comments with justifiable indignation on the number of male commentators who have extracted only what they wanted to see in these encounters!

Charles Rymer obviously found it a great mystery that God chose women to reveal the first news of His resurrection. He solved it by saying that women of course 'were being faithful to their womanly duties—they were at the tomb bringing spices for the body. This was a woman's work and so God honoured them because of their faithful performance of the responsibilities of their sex'! There is no evidence that this was a womanly task, but then this is typical of male commentators on the Gospel narrative—they see what they want to see! Dorothy Sayers comments, 'I have never heard a sermon preached on the story of Martha and Mary which did not attempt somehow to explain away the text. Mary's, of course, was the better part—the Lord said so and we must not contradict Him—but we will be careful not to despise Martha; no doubt He approved of her too. We could not get on without her and indeed we greatly prefer her for Martha was doing a really feminine job whereas Mary was being like any other disciple'!

While it is easy to be either cynical or greatly offended by the attitude of some Christian men down the ages and even today, we must keep our eyes firmly fixed on what God is actually saying to us as women and learn to turn the other cheek. Attitudes *are* gradually changing and we must follow our own guidance for today, forgetting about the rest.

Perhaps we should take courage from the Chinese church, which is emerging with some drive after the traumatic events of the Cultural Revolution. Before China became Communist, women were still totally subject to their menfolk, with the threefold law of obedience to their fathers, to their husbands and even to their sons! Today, having received equality at the hands of the Communists (and what an indictment that is!) women are playing a leading role in the revival of the Chinese church—accepted, respected and even receiving ordination.

3. True Femininity

Supporters of women's lib always give me the impression that they wish they had been born as men. Yet a fascinating study of some of the most successful women in the country, undertaken by a popular magazine, revealed that they had succeeded in their work not only because of their ability, but also because they had seen *the value of being a woman in that situation*—not, as women's lib would say, in spite of that misfortune! Our femininity can give us an enormous advantage.

We are equal in the sight of God but we are also different and complementary to our menfolk—and personally I can only say *vive la difference*!

Now the trouble is that whenever one makes this kind of observation a number of alarm bells start to ring in many Christian minds, because the subject of sexuality is an uncomfortable one for some people.

It is only a slightly unfair generalization to say that many Christians would feel happier if sexuality were seen in flat mid-grey tones, and all such feelings of mutual interest or appreciation between the sexes were cast into outer darkness! But to me this is to miss out on a large area of God-given and perfectly permissible colour in our world.

Of course we would all condemn the ugly and overt sexuality displayed on third-rate cinema hoardings and dragged sickeningly before us on our television screens, as yet another unmarried couple leap enthusiastically into bed together. But this is a far cry, surely, from ordinary everyday relationships between the sexes in the humdrum events of life? God has made us as we are, both male and female, and surely it is reasonable to suppose that He meant us to interact naturally in our lives and not to feel guilty the minute we begin to appreciate someone of the opposite sex simply for being as he or she is.

Sadly, the problem that many women experience in accepting their own sexuality often begins right back in childhood and in that very vital relationship with fathers and brothers in the family home.

Marion is a rather severely dressed lady in her mid-thirties who is struggling to survive as a teacher in a large comprehensive school. Although she is quite a gifted teacher, she is sure that no one really appreciates her ability. And certainly the headmaster and many of the other male teachers find her very prickly and after each encounter are usually left wondering what it is they have done wrong this time!

As a child, Marion suffered from a very over-critical father who made it extremely obvious that he preferred her younger brother. No matter how hard she tried, nothing she did was ever right whilst her brother, who was very far from being any kind of saint, could do no wrong in his father's eyes.

This in itself was bad enough, but then as Marion began growing up into a not unattractive young woman, the situation changed dramatically for the worse. Relations between her parents had never been good, and now, whenever Marion was alone in the house with her father, he suddenly began to lavish a great deal more attention on her than he had ever done in the past. She found this difficult enough to cope with, but on top of this, jealousy on the part of her mother made life even more unbearable. So Marion learned very early in life to feel guilty about being a woman and to shut off much of her femininity. Today she dresses severely and sensibly and avoids anything but the most cerebral and spiritual contacts with the opposite sex. But, sadly, she does not feel secure in her other gifts either. She knows that she is intelligent but, because of the criticism and jealousy she grew up with, she constantly feels unaccepted even in this area of her life. Though others in the school would gladly accept her for her ability, she feels she must fight and push to be recognized. And because she does this in a very unfeminine and aggressive manner, regarding every man as a potential threat to her identity, she alienates even those who have tried to accept her.

Every woman, married or single, needs the love and acceptance of the menfolk around her if she is to develop her femininity and appreciate her identity as a woman. Femininity is a response to a good experience of men; it does not exist in a vacuum. Where there is a loving and accepting father-daughter relationship in which the father encourages his daughter to make the best of herself and to relate in a normal healthy way to his appreciation of her femininity, then there are seldom any problems later in life.

But, if, as in Marion's case, the relationship is warped, the problems are carried on unresolved into adult life. The battle goes on, although the field of battle may have changed.

Marion feels she has to compete with the men at work because of her deep sense of non-acceptance as a woman. Her constant prickly defensiveness, not to mention her neurotic need to compete, are quickly making sure that her suspicion that she is not accepted becomes a fact!

But if, on the other hand, a woman has the love and acceptance of her father, her brothers and her husband, without being 'put down' in any way, then she feels secure to move forward as a woman into whatever area God would have her use her gifts. For instance, I have observed over and over again that the great majority of women who succeed in any area of life, whilst still retaining their femininity, be it as Prime Minister or secretary, wife or businesswoman, have one characteristic in common—they were loved and encouraged by their fathers to make the best of themselves and to use their gifts to the full.

What is femininity anyway?

To attempt actually to define femininity is like trying to hold half a pint of water in your hands without a proper container; it is so elusive that half of its substance escapes the minute you attempt to put words around it. For instance, one could say that a woman is warm, loving and intuitive, but many men possess similar qualities without becoming remotely effeminate.

Moreover, it completely misses the point to imply that a woman is only feminine if her aim in life is to be a wife and mother, if she does not participate in any job that brings her into competition with men and if she contents herself with making the tea or cleaning the brass. This indeterminate quality can neither be created by nor limited by any role.

I believe that it is possible to maintain our femininity in almost any walk of life where our gifts have led us, whether that be at the kitchen sink or on the Government front bench.

If we ask the question of some men, 'What do you find unfeminine and difficult to cope with in women?' we get some very interesting replies which are actually highly biblical.

The protection factor

The Bible teaches that a woman should be dependent on her husband as protector and indeed, nothing makes a man lose his sense of masculinity more quickly than a woman who appears to be totally self-sufficient. She may be clever, quick-witted or very able in a variety of different ways but if she appears not to need or even want the help of the men in her life, then they experience her as basically unfeminine. So femininity has very little to do with ability but a great deal to do with attitudes.

And, of course, the corollary is equally true—women need the love and support of their menfolk. Even when a woman reaches quite high levels in her career, she will probably still be more emotionally vulnerable than her male equivalent; this is simply a natural and desirable part of being feminine.

But suppose a woman finds that her husband or her boss is not supportive? Suppose he does not want to take the lead or expects her to cope alone without his help? Then she is forced into this unfeminine position anyway. It is not possible to be feminine if one is not given loving and supportive masculine headship. Very often when men point to a woman who is apparently dominant in her marriage and seems to be very unfeminine they need to look a little beyond the woman to find the cause of the situation.

A woman like Marion may have experienced so much unacceptance and criticism from the men in her life that she is *unable* to believe that anyone cares about her enough to want to help or protect her. Life with father or brothers may have been such a constant struggle for survival that she feels the fight must go on and any other man is just as likely to hurt her or let her down. Independence is then the only means of survival and inter-relationship a constant battle to prove that one is better or of real value. Perhaps I should add, in fairness, that male chauvinists also originate from the same stable! Show me a genuine chauvinist and I will show you a man whose dominant over-powerful mother constantly made him feel small and unaccepted.

Unfortunately, many blocks to real Christian love and acceptance lie not so much in particular and over-literal interpretations of Scripture, as in the early years of family life. To use a phrase which I coined in my last book on marriage, one has to ask, 'Who wrote the script?' Much of our behaviour originates from early family struggles and die-stamped behaviour patterns that have become so much a part of us that we are quite unaware of them.

Equal but different

Another way in which men experience women as unfeminine occurs when they feel that women are trying to be equal *and the same* as their menfolk rather than equal and different. More often than not this happens when women have felt rejected by their fathers and are still trying desperately to prove themselves to be as good as or better than men. But of course it is one thing to understand the root cause and another to handle this lovingly.

I have seen not a few women like this completely transformed by the love of husbands who took seriously their Christ-like responsibility within the marriage. Love does indeed cover all things and this kind of accepting, overcoming love can equally be given to the single woman within our churches, and job situations to restore to her a good feminine self-image.

But this is extremely unlikely to happen when discrimination exists against talented women inside and outside the church. When a woman knows that she is every bit as gifted and maybe even more so than her male counterparts, but is not allowed to use those gifts because she is 'only a woman', then she is scarcely likely to feel positive about being feminine! And it is at this point that the ugly and unfeminine, 'I'm as good as you are', struggle inevitably begins.

But when a woman is accepted in those positions for which her gifts equip her, and has no personal blocks against behaving in an ordinary feminine way, then the equality struggle never gets started. Indeed, as the survey I mentioned earlier in this chapter shows, the most successful women are those who have used their feminine gifts to the full, demonstrating that they are equal but different and complementary to their menfolk, in whatever situation they find themselves.

Sources of anxiety about being feminine

Often parents can actually instil a fear of being feminine in their children. Anxiety about sex, the feeling that it is some kind of horrendous and unchristian, wholly undesirable part of life, transmits itself to the children—so much so, in fact, that it shows itself in a high degree of sexual unfulfilment in many married Christian women. As one social worker commented recently, 'It's a wonder that any little baby Christians are ever born!' and in ordinary everyday life this fear emerges in some rather 'uptight' Christian ladies, who are more than a little afraid of their own sexuality.

Personally, I find this unnatural Christian attitude to sex very sad. Over and over again I have come across women who are frightened and ashamed to be feminine. This shows itself in how they dress, in their attitude to the men they meet and in their sex life. But, worst of all, it affects the way they bring up their own daughters to cope with boy/girl relationships.

I can absolutely understand that in the current climate of opinion, when free sex is paraded at large, worried parents of teenage girls are apt to be driven more and more into over-protective attitudes and actions. One thing that concerns me is that this is leaving in its wake a trail of frightened little girls who are terrified of their own sexuality—and who have frequently no one with whom they can discuss this in an honest way.

If Christianity is seen as a religion that frowns on sex and provides nothing but a series of 'don'ts' about normal human relationships, then we are not achieving a great deal. Surely our ideal can be found in Jesus who appreciated the women among His followers and accepted their femininity without any trace of anxious, tense monasticism. Herein lies our pattern to be able to appreciate each other's sexuality in a relaxed and normal kind of way, without getting obsessed about the problems and difficulties which do undoubtedly surround us.

Finally, there is the whole question of how we dress and make the best of our feminine attributes. Christians seem to be so guilt-ridden in this area that it has needed something like the American best-seller *The Total Woman* to get us thinking on this subject—even though some of Mrs Morgan's ideas are more than slightly outrageous!

All men appreciate a woman who takes trouble with her appearance and a dull, dowdy exterior is more likely to be seen by them as unfeminine and uninteresting than as godly, economical or modest. Life around us has taken on a technicolour quality and while, as Christians, we may not wish to go all the way with this, it is stupid to ignore it. For years I had at the back of my mind an awful picture of 'holy and Godly matrons' looking like a regiment of flat-heeled ladies with sensible tweedy skirts and scraped back hair—and I fear this is a caricature of church women that still lingers on for many outsiders today!

Certainly, as 1 Peter 3 says, the inner beauty of a woman is more important than the outer appearance, but that does not mean that we should give no time or attention to how we look. Many women at the time Peter was writing spent literally hours braiding their hair and dressing themselves up. Whilst this was clearly a wrong use of their time, there is no doubt in my mind that our menfolk would appreciate our paying a little bit more attention to our appearance than some Christian women have traditionally done!

4. The Married Woman

Getting married is so much the ultimate dream of most women that many enter the state of wedded bliss more than slightly unprepared for what lies ahead. Rather like the beautiful princess, riding off on a white charger with her newly-found Prince Charming, expecting to live happily ever after, the newly-married woman will be fairly unaware of what this new relationship will actually mean in practice in the cold, clear light of day!

All the talk and the preparation is geared towards the one great day and the marriage service itself and little or no teaching is given about the relationship of the couple—or how to build on this and help it grow. There are lists of guests, lists of wedding presents, plans for the honeymoon and plans for the house but seldom do they hear about how to build their future together so that they will still be happy in twenty years' time.

As Christians, we will probably be told that Christ must be at the centre of our lives together and that we must put Him first, but again, quite what this involves in practice easily gets lost in a glorious spiritual haze. Indeed, people are often left with the impression that they must put their Christian work outside the home before their families, thus adding another burden to the relationship. A Christian couple I counselled only last year had never heard a single sermon or even had half an hour's marriage preparation about building a good relationship together. Afterwards the husband said to me, 'But why, when we got married in church and have attended services faithfully for years, has no one ever told us what Christian marriage actually involved?'

Quite why this situation exists remains a mystery to me but I can only assume that it has something to do with the fairytale dreams of childhood and the myth that when two people who love each other get married they will automatically live happily ever after.

Sadly, statistics show that Christian marriages, especially among the clergy, are almost as much at risk as those in the world outside. Christians do tend to put their Christian work first at the expense of the relationship, and also they often seem to have a rather naive belief that if they are Christians, then nothing can go wrong.

Moreover, since Christians are rightly aware of the sanctity of marriage, if the relationship does begin to go wrong they are often embarrassed to look for help. A marriage counsellor with a telephone ministry in the West Country told me recently that callers who confessed to being Christians were reluctant to give their names for fear of what others might think. There is usually a great sense of guilt in admitting to any marital problems, however small, a fact which, not surprisingly, only serves to compound the original difficulty.

What principles must guide a Christian woman

trying to make a good marriage and stick to it?

Companionship is the first reason the Bible gives for the institution of marriage and it is still the most valuable one. 'The Lord God said, "It isn't good for man to be alone; I will make a companion for him, a helper suited to his needs"' (Genesis 2:18). When the first flush of love's excitement has passed and life has returned to a more even keel, the relationship itself and the quality of the time spent together must be the key to the success or failure of a marriage.

All scriptural teaching centres on this togetherness of husband and wife. These days we hear a great deal about wives submitting to their husbands, but the passage on marriage in Ephesians 5 verse 21 actually opens with these words: 'Honour Christ by submitting *to one another*.'

For a single woman, coming into this relationship fresh from a life of finding her own way in the world, with loving parents waiting anxiously in the wings, marriage is a complete change of direction. Suddenly her horizon has changed shape and this new world centres around the needs and aspirations of the one man she has chosen. Everything from now on is to be focused on this single relationship 'for richer, for poorer, for better, for worse'.

The Bible teaching of 'one flesh' in marriage is, I believe, meant to be taken a great deal more seriously than is customary these days. Most married people would say that they live as couples but actually they are living together under the same roof more as married single people. Sometimes you can almost see them pulling away at the ends of the marriage tie that binds them, each seeking their own interests and almost competing with one another for their slice of the cake. Certainly, in the world around us, marriage is seen only as another stage in the search for personal fulfilment, to be abandoned at will if the relationship does not work out, and certainly not worth making any real sacrifice for.

From the moment of marriage on, we have to be seeking each other's best interests, the things that unite rather than divide. Together we form a new identity that is 'us', not the wife falling over backwards to do what the husband wants, or vice versa, but the two of us together bound up in our love for God and for each other.

Speaking the truth in love

With couples where togetherness has really been worked at over the years, you can almost see this single identity emerging. Perhaps she begins to sound like him when she speaks and he may talk about her a lot in a way that shows how much she means to him. But as I know only too well from years of counselling, this 'togetherness' hardly ever 'just happens' as so many people seem to believe. It has to be worked at and worked at quite hard!

One of the most successful and 'together' couples I know started work on this during their honeymoon. Very early on she realized that his picture of married bliss, sitting happily behind the newspaper during breakfast, absorbed in lengthy and boring silences for much of the day, was not at all what she had in mind! Happily for her, she already knew from her own parents' marriage what a really good relationship could be like, and she set out with a will to bring this into her own marriage.

By the end of the honeymoon he was already saying that he really could not imagine why he had ever married her...but today, some twenty years later, they have forged a bond together and an ever-deepening love for one another that has stood the test of time and a good many trials.

Alas, many other people have kept silent at such times, simply wishing their marriage partners were different, but not doing or saying anything about their feelings. We may push these thoughts to the bottom of our 'thinking piles' but this will not make them go away!

Communication is the name of the game—and unfortunately for those who find it difficult, there is no other name. Sadly, so many women who have set out on marriage with great hopes of love and under-standing have never risked actually telling their husbands what they really need from them.

Almost every woman carries into her marriage hopes and expectations of her partner that she has probably never even verbalized. Sometimes they are only little things, but they matter. Really, if we are honest with ourselves, we must see that there is no way that our husbands can know what these expecta-tions are unless we talk about them openly and clearly. What usually happens is a state of silent resentment *after* he has omitted whatever it was that he was supposed to have known! How much better to talk about this openly and tell him the things that really matter to us, giving him the chance to meet our needs—rather than blaming him because he hasn't!

Submission to one another

As so many marriages around us have been breaking up, some Christians have gone rushing to their Bibles in a frantic search for an instant solution: Marriage

Cure—Take Whole Bottle, Wife to Submit to Husband. (Full stop!)

The trouble is that the teaching on submission is usually taken out of context and preached as a cure for all marital problems. Quite apart from being scripturally unsound and unbalanced, this one-sided instruction amounts to psychological suicide. Of course if you give one physically stronger partner in the marriage everything he wants whenever he wants it in the name of 'scriptural obedience' then the relationship will be all sweetness and light in his eyes—we all like to have our own way! But is this what Scripture is saying on the subject? Personally, I believe it is a complete travesty of the truth and dishonouring to the God who made us.

The actual teaching on submission in Ephesians 5 is very different. 'Honour Christ by submitting *to each other*. You wives must submit to your husbands' leadership in the same way as you submit to the Lord, for a husband is in charge of his wife in the way that Christ is in charge of his body, the church. He gave his very life to take care of it and be its Saviour (Ephesians 5:21–23).

All instructions to wives on submission must pale into insignificance in the light of these awe-inspiring directions to husbands, who are to be the very type of Christ within the relationship. When loving leadership such as this is given, submission and obedience must surely take on a very different aspect.

Submission *to one another,* with the husband cast in the role of ultimate decision-maker and protector, is the ideal for Christian marriage and this mutual submission is intended to be a kind of visual aid of Christ's love for the church—our relationship is literally to show Christ's love in the world around us.

Identity

One frequent casualty in this misunderstanding of a wife's role has been the wife's sense of identity and feeling of self-worth within the marriage relationship. Who are you? Oh, just somebody's wife!

Whilst it is true that we are to work at becoming a genuine partnership this is not supposed to happen at the expense of one or other marriage partner.

Each of us is called to be so concerned with the other's needs and aspirations that we devote our time and our prayers to building each other up. To quote Dr Jack Dominian:

> In today's world, we can and should expect our partners to help us grow as people—each seeking to understand the other's world of fears and fantasies and to respond to the other's needs. We expect our marriage partners to provide the means of healing the wounds of the past—the rejecting parent needs to be replaced by the accepting spouse; our previous lack of self-esteem to be replaced by our marriage partner's love and approval.

In counselling I come across many men who have had their sense of self-worth virtually destroyed by the continual criticism and non-acceptance of their wives, and even more women who have felt so trammelled by their husband's demands that they have lost all sense of their own value and identity. When this happens in a Christian marriage the tragedy is compounded as it is such a clear denial of the very purpose for which marriage was intended.

A married woman needs to feel that her husband values her for more than just her cooking or her housekeeping. As the writer of Proverbs realized, her longing is to know that she herself is 'a pearl of great price' in her husband's eyes.

We have already seen that much of the work that a married woman has to do is devalued in the eyes of the world. In leaving home, she has lost the readily available love and affection of her parents, and when she stops work to have children, she will also lose the encouragement of job satisfaction together with the feeling that she is of value in the outside world. From that moment on, she depends almost entirely on her husband for that vital sense of self-worth, without which none of us can survive.

I meet so many women who grind their way through the days with no sense of value and no spark of interest left in them. Their own identity is totally submerged in that of their husbands and their children and they live in dread of what will happen when the children leave home.

Certainly becoming a wife and mother involves a very real sacrifice, but we are not meant to drown ourselves utterly in the process! The perfect wife in Proverbs had a good many outside interests to keep her feeling involved—and, incidentally, to give her something to talk to her husband about!

It seems to me that this is an area where Christian women frequently misunderstand the teaching on being married. Almost enthusiastically they rush to the altar to lay themselves down like some kind of female doormat for their husbands to walk over.

But surely it is reasonable to suppose that a wife's husband chose her in the first place because of the kind of person she was in her own right—not because of what she might become when totally submerged as his wife! If a husband comes home at night after an interesting, stimulating day at work he is surely very unlikely to be inspired by yet another speech on how tiresome the children have been, or why the washing machine is not working properly. Of course she will need to share this with him and, hopefully, he will respond helpfully and lovingly, but companionship demands more than this. I believe we have a duty, not only to ourselves but to our husbands, to keep alive some outside interest and to be informed about what is going on in the world. The mutual companionship that is meant to lie at the centre of marriage is not really possible with the non-participation of one sleeping partner, who is so engrossed with the problems of home and children that she does not really want to know!

Losing our sense of self-worth will also affect how we dress and the way we look to other people. As Christians, we are probably particularly vulnerable here. Because we are, rightly, always giving to others in greater need than ourselves, and because we are aware of the quite high cost of looking nicely turned out, this is often a priority that gets pushed to the bottom of the list. Equally, our husbands may not realize how much money it requires to look good and dress attractively. Like everything else in our lives, this requires open and honest discussion and perhaps even a visit to the shops together.

Helping one another through life

Chapter 31 of Proverbs says of the perfect wife that her husband can trust her and she will richly satisfy all his needs. She will not hinder him but help him all the days of her life.

From the moment a man gets married, he will probably have very little time or opportunity for friendship or fellowship outside his home. The sheer pressure of a working day combined with travelling to and fro will usually take up all of his time and much of his energy too. A married woman on the other hand, unless she is working full time, will very likely have the support and encouragement of other friends in the neighbourhood.

It is quite probable that a husband will be depending almost entirely on his wife for friendship and support. Her love and her encouragement are the springboard from which he leaves home in the morning, refreshed and strengthened to face the new day with all its problems. Over and over again in counselling, I am saddened to realize how little Christian couples understand of this aspect of their lives together. The wife may have spent some time concentrating on what to cook for supper and had a quick flip round to see that the house is tidy, but offers nothing more than a cursory, 'Did you have a good day, dear?' on the subject of his life's work.

Similarly, he will almost certainly return home full of the day's problems, desperate to fling himself into the nearest chair and switch on the TV, and will pay little more than lip-service to the need to enquire about his wife's day. Probably both of them will then have to rush out again to some Christian meeting!

In all the rush of everyday life there is a very great danger of spending what little time we have together skating irrelevantly over the surface of things and never sitting down to talk about how each of us really feels and what our actual needs are.

It is amazing how, at the very moment my husband returns home from work, the telephone starts to ring, a saucepan appears about to boil over and one or other of the children demands immediate help with chemistry homework that I don't begin to understand! Without very careful planning, this time of the day can rapidly deteriorate into total chaos and bad feeling all round! We have found in our family that it is essential to set aside time in which we consciously sit down and talk together. And by this I mean really talk about how we feel, rather than about the clutter and busyness that normally fills up our lives. Perhaps it is worth saying that this sort of conversation does not come easily to the average Englishman and that we have had to learn to share and help one another in this way.

So often it seems that couples only talk about the surface concerns in their lives, and this is true even in their prayer times together. They talk of the children, the church, the garden or even the work they are doing, but only in terms of what has happened or what action they should take, nothing more. The fact that this may be making them feel pressurized, or rejected, or unloved, hardly ever gets mentioned except in a crisis. But surely it is our feelings and our reactions to things that make up what we are inside, and if we cannot relate or pray about what is happening at this level then we are not even beginning to meet each other's needs.

Another important factor in the relationship is that of building one another up. It is amazing how readily the negative criticisms about our husbands or wives seem to spring to mind whilst the positively encouraging things never even get mentioned.

One husband said to me recently that his wife had a great gift for spotting the things that he had forgotten to do or not done very well, whilst in all their married life she had never once mentioned her appreciation of the money he brought home or the house he had provided and furnished for the family

—all that was apparently to be taken for granted!

Again, far too many women whose marriages are not going very well find themselves gossipping around amongst their friends to the point of disloyalty, whilst never actually talking to their husbands about the problem, or to someone who could help them.

Because there is so little understanding of how a husband and wife can help each other to become a really united couple, I honestly believe that many married people are missing out in their relationships where they do not need to. The Bible speaks of marriage as an illustration of Christ's love for the church, and clearly the family unit is the cornerstone of our society, so surely we must do all we can to improve the quality of our lives in this area.[1]

[1] For those who want to follow up this subject in greater detail, I have covered this in my book *Marriage in the Balance*.

5. Motherhood

While our teenage daughters sit huddled over their O-level and A-level exam papers, chewing their pencils desperately in an attempt to remember the exact wording of some scientific theory or the right date of the Treaty of Utrecht, there is one certain factor that we can take for granted about their education—they will have had little or no teaching for the life of a wife and mother that lies ahead of the great majority of them.

One woman told me recently that there were days when she honestly wished she had never gone to university. She had found that time of her life so interesting and stimulating that now the stark contrast of struggling to cope with three little children in a small terraced house was almost more than she could cope with.

To me, the terrifying irony of this hole in our education system is the fact that very little in our lives is likely to be more important than bringing up these small human beings entrusted to our care. Their whole future, their sense of self-worth, their view of life and even the quality of their faith—everything—depends on how good a job we make of these few short years of motherhood.

But sadly the only education that many of us will have received on this most vital of subjects came as we grew up in our homes. Since one in three homes are currently broken by divorce, this does not augur well for the future of our society.

We learn from our mothers and we copy them far more closely than we ever realize. From our mothers we acquire behaviour patterns that are so much a part of us that we perform them instinctively, automatically accepting what was done as 'right' and what was not as 'wrong'. Even if we consciously reject these patterns, we will still have very little idea of how to behave any differently! If the experience of being 'mothered' was a good and loving one with enough acceptance and encouragement, then there is, of course, no problem. But what if it was not?

On being a mother

I will never forget the extraordinary sensation of going into hospital as one and coming out as two separate individuals. Watching my tiny daughter lying beside me in the cot gave me a simultaneous feeling of wonder and of panic. How on earth was I to cope? Would I do it right? Who would advise me? However, by the time our second and third children came along, I had learnt to relax and follow my God-given instincts about their needs. In the beginning we worry far too much about doing the right thing and it is common knowledge that, alas, we nearly always make our mistakes on the first child!

There are so many simultaneously good and unnerving experiences involved in becoming a mother. There is the celebration and thanksgiving and

49

wonder but also the feeling of being more than slightly unprepared for what lies ahead. Much as we want our children there is very likely a sense in which we have not wholly counted the cost beforehand.

Once a family has started, there is very obviously no turning back! We cannot simply put little Johnny in cold storage so that we can have a week or two on our own to catch up with some sleep or to do something that we really want to do. The chances are that life with tiny children, once started, will go on for a good eight to ten years and then, although the responsibilities become less all-pervading, they go on in a different and frequently more demanding way, for at least another ten or fifteen years!

Of course, none of us who have had the blessing of children would want it any other way, because actually they are around for a surprisingly short time and we miss them terribly when they go—but it just does not seem like this when the children are tiny and very demanding and whole nights of sleep are a thing of the past.

As one mother with three tiny children said to me recently—'It would be all right if I thought there would be anything left of me at the end of all this.'

In one very real sense mother love and the giving of ourselves for our children, is the epitome of Christian sacrifice. It is quite out of tune with the search for rights and identity that is the hallmark of our age. Many times in the Bible, mother love is held up by God as supreme above all other earthly loves.

So what happens if we find ourselves simply unable to give this love—and indeed almost resentful that it should be asked of us?

Jenny Rivers grew up in a home where the only things that mattered were good exam results and success at school. Her mother taught in the local grammar school and was always too busy to spend time with the children or make them feel wanted. Instead of love, Jenny was aware of one thing—that she and her younger sisters were really a nuisance and the cause of a great deal of extra work to their parents. In addition, as Jenny was not very clever, she always felt that she had no real value in her mother's eyes. She grew up feeling a total failure and eventually married the first man who asked her, because at least he seemed to want her for herself.

But now Jenny is stuck at home with two tiny children of her own and life is almost worse than before. Jenny thought she wanted children, but with two little boys under three years old—totally and drainingly dependent on her all day and every day—she feels that she will sink without trace. What little identity she had managed to find before the children came along seems to have gone for ever. What is worse, she has no idea how to cope or to give them the love that she never received herself. Her husband, Brian, is devoted to his sons and finds her attitude incomprehensible. How could she possibly not love these beautiful children? And so once again Jenny feels a failure. She has no idea why everything has gone wrong, and longs only to get the children away to school so she can get back to some kind of work where she can prove to someone, and to herself, that she has some real value!

The problem with Jenny and with many young mothers who have not found their identity before or during the early days of marriage, is that they find themselves having to surrender everything before they are nearly ready to do so. Often they have been prepared more for good exam results or an interesting and stimulating job than for this very earthy and demanding career of motherhood.

If a woman is already secure in her own identity, and feels loved within the marriage relationship, then she is able to lay down her life and gladly put her career and other interests into cold storage for six or eight years. But if she is not, then the years ahead may well be unhappy ones, fraught with bitterness and resentment, that do more harm than good to the young lives entrusted to her.

So, whilst it is often frowned upon by potential grandparents and older Christian folk, I personally think there is a great deal to be said for a woman carrying on her career, or simply enjoying married life alone with her husband, for as many years as it takes for her to find her own sense of value and identity within the relationship. The same is just as true for husbands who often experience their wives' devotion to the children as a 'taking away' from their own sense of worth within the relationship. Many women are now starting families at around twenty-nine or thirty and find themselves far more able to love and cope with the children as a result.

If the husband and wife are truly listening to one another's needs, and able to give each other the emotional and spiritual input that is so vital in these years, then there will be few problems anyway. But so often the pressures of time and tiredness prevent us discussing areas of hurt and deprivation in the relationship. Does the wife feel that she has been quite literally 'left with the baby', while her husband passes by on the other side, more interested and involved in his work and in the church than in her welfare? Has he realized that the need to give her the Christ-like love and support that 1 Peter speaks of is greater at this time than at any other? Alternatively, does the husband feel that now that the children have come along, his wife no longer loves or needs him? These issues need talking through and facing up to as they arise and not months or years later when the unspoken accusations have caused a permanent rift.

The current secular view has devalued mother-hood. We have been conditioned to see anything we do in the home, whether it be as a wife or a mother, as being only second-rate and of no intrinsic value. But consider the tremendous potential there is in this aspect of a woman's career.

The child's whole personality and sense of well-being is affected totally by the love and attention that his mother gives or witholds from him in the first few months and years of his life. If she holds him and looks at him with eyes of love then he will sense his own worth and want to respond to her and to others around him positively. But if she leaves him alone to cry, spending only that time that is essential with him and attending to his physical needs in a cold and businesslike way, he will begin to feel that he has no real value in her eyes, that he is just a nuisance and should apologize for his very existence. Sadly, it is all too easy for a psychiatrist or counsellor to guess accurately the quality of mothering that people have had, so clear is this in their own self-image in later life.

So great is our responsibility as mothers that we can even determine the quality of our children's spiritual lives. Parents are, I believe, intended to be visual aids of God to the children entrusted to them, but if a mother is never there when needed or too busy to care about his needs and fears, then we can expect him to project these same attitudes on to God.

This is an awesome responsibility that we neglect at our children's peril!

Acceptance

If there is one word that we should inscribe on our hearts in connection with motherhood it is the simple word 'acceptance'. Of course discipline and hard work matter and of course we long for our children to grow up to embrace the faith that we hold as Christians, but if we do not put loving acceptance of our children *as they are* before everything, then all our efforts may be doomed to failure, because we will very likely drive them into resentment or open rebellion anyway!

If God accepts us as we are and if, while we were yet sinners, Christ died for us, then what right have we to pressurize our children into changing before we will lovingly accept them? Just as the people that Christ encountered were changed and convicted by His loving acceptance of them, so our children will only change if we love them *first,* however exasperating they may be at times—rather than offering our love as some kind of carrot that they will receive if they are good enough or work hard enough.

As for Jenny, her parents were unable to accept her because they themselves felt unloved and inadequate. They created a tense nervous atmosphere in which they tried to pressurize their children to succeed where they had failed. It is a vicious circle which continues until someone like Jenny is helped to see what she is doing to her children.

Communication

Closely linked with acceptance is the fraught subject of communication. Over the years I have met so many mothers who find they cannot talk to their children that it is really quite frightening. Actually what is happening is a gradual non-acceptance that builds up throughout childhood—starting when a young boy tries to tell his mother that 'he really hates that nasty little boy next door'—or that he is bored to tears with Sunday school. A horrified look or a well-meaning 'You know the Bible tells us to love our enemies' is enough to starve out these little confidences at the outset. Probably the mother thinks that she has done her *Christian* duty but actually she has erected a large red warning light about saying what she really feels!

Later on, when the question in his mind is, 'How can you possibly believe in God, when the teacher says the world all evolved by itself?' or, 'My friend went shop-lifting yesterday and he wants me to go with him next time', there is considerably less chance that he will risk asking it. And so the gap gets bigger until the situation is far more desperate than the sublimely ignorant mother probably ever realizes.

All the questions and problems that come up daily at school are never aired. Other girls sleep with their boyfriends; at the party down the road she gets offered pot and everyone else is trying it—but she dare not discuss the problems openly at home for fear of moralizing disapproval. Meanwhile mother and father are busy lamenting together about how impossible it is to talk to teenagers these days!

In a short chapter on motherhood it is clearly not possible to go into this subject more fully but the number one priority for any mother trying to build up and keep open the channels of communication with her children is to learn to listen and to accept. Never say 'Oh! you shouldn't feel like that' because the simple fact of the matter is that he does, or he would not be telling you! If he feels that you are with him in whatever experience he is trying to tell you about, then he will risk it again another time.

If you feel that something you know or believe might be helpful, offer it in an open-handed, adult to adult, way after you have accepted what he says. Don't come down from a great judgemental parent to child height—Mother has spoken, end of subject!

For example, when talking about the nasty, spiteful little girl at school, after first accepting that this *is* what he feels about her, it might be helpful to talk about the reasons why children sometimes behave like this. Do you think she is unhappy at home? Could it be that she is getting at you because she is jealous? Shall we pray for her and for you in coping with it? If the feeling is really boiling up you can often help your child get it down to size by a simple acting out that hurts nobody.

Years ago now a neighbour's child who was in the same form as one of my children kept on needling away at her and teasing her to such an extent that she found the situation almost unendurable. All attempts to talk it through and pray about it seemed doomed to failure and in the end I decided some action was called for. We got a large and rather battered cushion from the playroom, called it Nicola, put it on the floor and told her to do whatever she wanted with it. A seraphic smile spread over her face as she set to work pummelling and kicking the cushion until all the anger and bitterness was exhausted. When she had finished, the problem had somehow come down to size. I scarcely ever heard about Nicola again.

Making time

So often mothers imagine that they must 'do something marvellous' in order to be worthwhile mothers —run fantastic parties, answer all the right questions, make the home really nice or cook the most marvellous food. Certainly, our consumer society would have us believe that the only things that really matter are hamburgers, sweets, expensive toys and days out! But actually the most important thing about a mother is that she is there and that she cares.

Making time for the child who wants to talk, listening to his problems and letting him do things with you—even if he makes a mess of it—are far more vital than anything else.

Many people I have counselled over the years never really knew a good relationship with their mothers because marvellous meals, a beautifully kept house or giving big presents were thought to be an adequate substitute—but there is no substitute for a Mum who loves and cares about you and makes the time to be with you, whether you want to talk or not.

6. The Working Wife

Freda Jones is a warm loving kind of person who really enjoys running a home full of children and animals. She is happy cleaning and polishing and doing the odd jobs that come up like arranging flowers in church and driving the old people to their fellowship meeting. Her house is constantly open to all-comers, and, without realizing this, Freda's love and hospitality have almost become the focal point of the whole area. For many years she has been quite contented living like this, but now, just as her children are beginning to leave home, Freda has a new neighbour who makes her feel totally inadequate. Despite her two children and numerous other commitments, Jane is like a power-house, organizing everything in sight and generally telling everybody else, including Freda, what they should be doing. Although she knows in her heart that there is no way she can compete with Jane, Freda is suddenly dissatisfied with her own life, wondering if she shouldn't be a better wife and mother, or a better organizer or something! All the insecurity she used to feel as a child in school comes racing up for attention and her whole contented world seems suddenly to have fallen around her.

Melanie is a young housewife struggling hard to keep her head above water with two tiny children in a small semi-detached house nearly two miles out of town on a brand-new housing estate. Before her marriage and for many months afterwards Melanie had an interesting job in the local shop that kept her occupied and contented. Though she loves her home and her children, the past few years have been a nightmare. Three-year-old Stephen arrived before she really wanted children and now, with two children under four, she feels well and truly trapped. Her husband, Mike, had never really liked her working and is very happy to have her safely tucked away at home. Brought up to believe that wives should stay at home, he seemed to experience her work as some kind of competition—a threat to his masculinity. Unfortunately, he was also brought up to believe that his role was solely as the breadwinner and head of the family so that the children he so desperately wanted have been left entirely to Melanie to look after—as well as the house! (Although he always notices if the place is untidy or the children are not in bed on time!) Melanie is young and very capable and she loves her husband, but is beginning to dislike his so-called 'Christian' attitudes more and more. Everything centres round his role on the PCC, in the Stewardship Campaign and in the church, while she is left struggling desperately to cope with many of the things around the house that a man would normally do. To begin with she filled this gap lovingly and made a real effort to achieve the submissiveness that he seemed to expect, but now that the giving seems to be almost all one way, her love is rapidly turning to resentment. She longs only for the children to reach school age so that she can return to work and recover some sense of worth—and if Mike objects to this, he is in for a rough time!

Jenny Robinson is a tall, elegant lady in her mid-forties who manages her home and family with apparent ease at the same time as she works as a local magistrate, and sits on a number of different committees in the area. In one sense, Jenny never actually stopped working even when the children were tiny for she was always interested in some project or other in the church, whether it was the PCC, organizing some kind of housegroup work or visiting the local prison. But when the children were finally all away at school she felt free to accept some of the outside offers that were beginning to come her way. Much as she loved her family and her home, the work was a real challenge to her and a breath of fresh air after the rather narrow confines of the house and parish.

While Jenny has found nothing but encouragement and acceptance from those she works with outside the home, it is sometimes a rather different story back in the parish. Her friends in the fellowship feel she has deserted them and are quick to question 'whether she is doing the right thing'. Her husband has been brought up to believe that a wife shouldn't work and, being slightly unsure of himself anyway, is more than a little threatened and is wondering where all this will lead. And just occasionally there are times when Jenny herself doesn't know where the next ounce of energy will come from—especially when everything happens at once in her life—running the home, trying to spend enough time with the children, as well as coping with all the other responsibilities in connection with her work. It can sometimes be quite a tricky balancing act! At times, she misses the loving supportive friends who used to understand her. What she usually gets nowadays is rather unloving criticism. If she is tired or ill, friends suggest in a rather pointed way that 'she shouldn't be doing so much' and if everything goes wrong the implication is that God must be trying to tell her something about working, when she has a family to bring up!

Sometimes Jenny finds this very hard. She knows that God has called her to the work she is involved with and she is well able to organize her home and family so that neither her husband nor her children suffer in any way from this. The work is very rewarding and the added interest in her life is helping her to take a much more positive look at her own identity. Yet at times the lack of friendship and Christian support in her life can be quite hard to cope with.

All wives and mothers 'work'—there can be no doubt in anyone's mind about that! As we cope with the piles of washing and ironing, housework and gardening, together with lovingly meeting the needs of our husband and children, it can be a pretty time-consuming and tiring existence. But, as I have said, the work that women find themselves doing as a normal part of being a wife and mother has been totally devalued: 'What do you do?' 'Oh! I'm only a housewife!' A woman like Freda, who has provided so much for the family in the way of love and support, washing and ironing, cooking and cleaning and on whom the security and strength of her whole family rests, is often made to feel nothing more than a glorified housekeeper!

Part of the pressure comes because society implies that women today can and should expect something much 'better' from their lives, but part of it also comes from exactly the source it should not—our own marriage partners. Melanie, for instance, has given up her job willingly to care for the home and children, but her husband with his lack of appreciation and affection, is actually busy destroying the very thing that he most needs.

It is not for nothing that the passage on the ideal wife in Proverbs 31 ends with these words 'Praise her for the many fine things she does; these good deeds of hers shall bring her honour and recognition from even the leaders of the nations.' One of today's greatest problems is that men have not given praise where it was due, but on the contrary, have taken the precious home-making and loving qualities of women and almost stamped them in the dust.

Working outside the home

To me the whole question 'to work, or not to work' outside the home is a matter for individual guidance only and should never be subject to what 'they' do or 'they' say. All the pressures on the three women mentioned above have come from outside themselves. Freda feels pressurized by her neighbour, Jenny by the criticism of Christians around her and Melanie by her husband's non-acceptance of her worth. But God has called us as *individuals* and we are accountable to Him for what we do with our lives, not to our neighbours and friends.

Listening to much of the current debate on the subject of women working, one would really think that the parable of the talents was written exclusively for men! The gifts of a married woman in particular, are, it seems, almost automatically to be cancelled out, rather as if she had lost every one of them the minute she stepped into her wedding dress!

And sadly, although much of the discussion rages

around certain negative verses of scripture, one has often a very strong feeling that the real problem lies much more in people's own fears and prejudices, than in a genuine attempt to get to grips with scriptural principles and real needs.

For instance, Jenny's husband, being a fairly insecure person, is probably much more concerned about what people will think of *him*, when his wife is working, than with Jenny's needs. Her friends in the parish feel that she has deserted them and want her back working with them at a level they can accept and understand. The very fact that she is able to do all she does and run a family, too, knocks at their own security and lack of identity.

So in all such discussion we need to be wholly honest with one another about what our fears and fantasies really are, rather than hiding behind convenient verses of scripture.

Instead of looking at Jenny and asking what her gifts are, and how she should be using them, both her husband and her friends are talking about the roles they feel she should be playing. But we have a God who says to us, 'I have graven you on the palms of my hands and the very hairs of your head are all numbered.' He loves and cares for each one of us as an individual creation. We are not a mass of typecast males or females, docilely playing what other people feel are our appointed roles! He loves us whether we are being used like Deborah the prophetess or like Martha, busy in the kitchen.

Working at home

Freda also has an identity problem. She feels her security threatened by Jane, and by those who extol

'Superwomen'. Memories of schooldays and of always being told she should 'try harder' or 'do better', flood into her consciousness and suddenly the contented life that God has called Freda Jones to live feels shaky and of no real value.

Very possibly she is exactly where God has called her to be but, like many of us, she is vulnerable to outside pressure and especially to organizing busybodies like Jane. Unfortunately, there seems to be something about certain Christians that makes them feel that they must try to change other people's lives rather than accepting them as they are in love. They are like the husband who marries intending to 'knock his partner into shape' and make her more like what he wants her to be! This is not the true love of Christ that comes acceptingly to each individual and changes us by the light of His loving presence alone.

Things are not always what they seem

Although men may, beforehand, be anxious about whether or not their wives should work, experience shows that they are often pleasantly surprised at the results.

One well-known Christian told me recently that he had just got a "new wife"—the change in his old one was so dramatic after she had finally taken the plunge and gone back into teaching. She was suddenly much more alive, more fulfilled and confident and he was reaping the benefit of it. The same has been true for another couple who used to go for counselling month after month with almost unending marriage problems—very largely because she depended entirely on what the relationship could give her when her husband returned home at night. Frankly, he was not able to match up to these expectations—it was too heavy a burden. She was also understretched at home. Now that she is out at work part time, she is a completely different and much more fulfilled woman, able to give much more to the relationship herself.

The parable of the talents—for women

A gifted woman, or one whom God wants to use in a wider field than her own home, is never going to feel fulfilled looking after the house and the cat seven or eight hours a day once the children are all at school. As we saw in a previous chapter, modern labour-saving devices and much smaller houses mean that housework is much less demanding and much less varied than it once was. Rather than looking at this negatively we should be positive. For example, as Jack Dominian said in a recent interview, the status of women today has at long last reached that envisaged in the Book of Genesis, when the man and the woman *were* equal before God!

So it really must follow that, once the children are at school, a woman will need to do something which uses her other talents in some way. If, like Jenny or Melanie, she needs to go out and use her talents in a wider area, then to frustrate this desire, either in the name of tradition or out of fear, will have a stultifying effect on her personality, and on the marriage relationship itself. Husbands who try to hold their wives back in this way have probably no idea how much richer the relationship can become once each of them has an interest to share with the other.

Work that brings in a little bit of extra cash and interest does not have to be all that high-powered or specialized. Quite a lot of women enjoy cleaning someone else's house for a couple of mornings a week—the scene is different, the families they work with provide extra interest and involvement, and other people's mess and dirt seems somehow easier and more manageable than their own!

Someone who likes ironing or cooking could try offering her services in the local paper. Alternatively, typing at home is a good standby, even for women with quite young children. Work of this kind seldom occupies more than a few hours a week, and it does not take us away from the family or from our Christian commitments either. It does, however, serve to broaden our interests and introduces us to people outside the confines of our family and church.

Working at home as a vocation

While some, like Jenny and Melanie, may need to work outside the home, a woman like Freda has already been greatly used in the parish to provide a 'home base' to which people can come. She is a natural homemaker and enjoys the work she does from there. Since she seems to have no real financial or emotional need to work, Freda is exactly the kind of woman who should remain at home and be a real blessing to others around her. If we really open our homes and our lives to God in this way, there is no limit to the way He can use us.

There are a very large number of voluntary associations which could not exist without the regular support of women who do not go out to work. From Meals on Wheels to the NSPCC and hospital visiting, not to mention all the Christian organizations, the world would be a much poorer place without the on-going care and support that many thousands of women give, year in and year out. And one of the dangers of women building their lives around only those activities that provide a bit of extra cash is, of course, that the voluntary organizations will find willing helpers harder and harder to come by.

Each of us has to answer before God for what we do with our lives and this may just as likely to be to go out to work as it may be to stay at home.

Going back to paid employment

One problem that the wife and mother who does go back to paid employment outside the home nearly always has to face is that of a loss of confidence and individual identity. She may not have been out much mixing with other people while her children were young. Her training, whatever that was, will seem very distant, and her work experience distinctly rusty. If her husband has not given her the loving support or 'input' that we all so badly need, she may also not feel that she has much to offer anyway. All this, and the sudden prospect of a much busier and more complicated life-style, running a job and a family together, will seem daunting indeed. Moreover, it would be naive to suppose that there are no other problems involved!

The ideal job for a married woman should consist of around three days a week with totally flexible hours preferably between nine and three-thirty, but find it if you can! There seems very little work available that is not either full-time or just very occasional and not a lot that takes account of school hours and holidays.

With the exception of teaching it is mainly the caring professions such as nursing, physiotherapy and medicine itself which offer such opportunities. Cleaning and typing, media or free-lance work are other options.

One of the best ideas I have heard of is the principle of work-sharing, where, for example, two wives agree together to act as secretary for the same employer, or district nurse for the same circuit, helping each other out with all the problems that come up like sick children and supermarket shopping.

I am more and more convinced that as Christians we are missing out in some of the more practical outworkings of community living. We all live our lives in little boxes, looking after our statutory two and a half kids, plus cooking, plus housework, while our neighbours and friends are struggling with identical problems and pressures often just a few hundred yards up the road!

One may be very gifted at cooking and decorating, while another actually enjoys keeping the house clean and tidy and a third would, if given the choice, spend the whole time looking after the children. Now surely it should be possible to harness these talents in some way without actually moving in together: to form one enormous community. Especially it should be possible to help those who are out working who cannot afford to pay for help.

One of the greatest problems facing wives with full-time jobs is that of sheer exhaustion. Unlike her husband, a married woman returns after a day's work to find several more hours of hard labour awaiting her. Breakfast dishes lie unwashed in the sink, the ironing glares at her from an enormous pile in the corner, and that night's chaos of homework is added to the previous day's residue on and around the table. Then the first thing she hears when she comes through the door is, 'What's for supper, Mum?'

Many women who work are desperate for every penny to help the family get by—but if it is at all possible, help with the housework is a life-saver for a working housewife. I could not possibly do without the friend who is at this very moment banging away at the typewriter for me, and another who helps me with the ironing and the housework. And there is a sense in which what is helping me is also helping them, since I am merely sharing the work around and using their talents as well as my own.

The trouble is that we have got so insular and so un-Christian in our thinking that managing our house 'on our own and without help' has become almost a matter of pride. 'I ought to be able to cope' has become the unspoken by-word of this generation. But is this Christian, when we have been taught to bear one another's burdens and share what we have (including work) with those in need? I very much doubt it!

Working clergy wives

Some clergy wives go out to paid employment either out of necessity or because they have a real gift that God is calling them to use. Obviously, they cannot afford to pass on part of what they earn to someone who will help in the house. Yet the housework has to be done, so the poor old vicar, who is technically 'around all day', has to add much of the housework to his already pressurized day. But is this not a case where some sort of 'parish talent bank' could come into operation, providing much-needed help, without payment, as a form of real giving?

There is always considerable resistance to the idea

of a 'talent bank' like this, especially when it comes to help in the house. Some years ago I wrote an article in the Church of England Newspaper, suggesting a community talent bank. It provided, for the most part, highly predictable replies—people wrote in to say that it was up to each one of us to manage our own homes, and that if a woman couldn't do this, she shouldn't be working! But there were a few really encouraging letters telling us of inspired talent and home-help schemes where individuals and in some cases whole parishes had got together to help each other out, and, incidentally, had benefited greatly from the love and fellowship that they had enjoyed in the process.

Life with a working wife and mother

Although a woman who works will undoubtedly bring more interest and a more healthy and relaxed self-image into the family, there are other areas where 'things certainly aint wot they used t'be'! Home-made puddings, beds made up and rooms tidied by Mum and washing all ironed and sorted, ready to use when the family needs it, are usually a thing of the past—if they were ever there in the first place! As one full-time editor said to me recently, 'I feel so guilty when I go out to dinner and realize that the wife has been slaving over the cooker all day to produce it!'

Organization is the name of the game

As a fairly disorganized person myself, I am constantly amazed at how much more I can get through in life when my time is put to the best advantage—and because I was not brought up in a very organized household either, these techniques have had to be picked up from other people and learnt the hard way, through bitter experience.

Work operates on the principle of Parkinson's Law. Just as the old lady staying in Brighton takes all day to write a few postcards because she has all day, so equally those same postcards can be written in half-an-hour or less if that is all the time available!

It is a well-known fact that if you want something done you ask an already busy person to do it because she is much more likely to know how to organize her time than the woman who is still getting into a state because she hasn't finished Monday's ironing yet!

Hints that I have found helpful

Shopping:
This really only needs to be done once a week except for the odd item, so plan it well ahead with a comprehensive list. This presupposes that you have already:

1. Made a menu for the week, writing down all that you will need for this.
2. Planned the times that you will bake or cook, during which you will *never* (except when really broke) make only one of anything but always two or three to put into the freezer compartment for a later and even more pressurized occasion.

Tidying up:
One friend I know gets the whole family to have a mass tidy up on a Sunday evening—I am still working on it but it sounds a great idea!

Lists:
Now that I have very little time to sit and think, lists

have become essential. A list made last thing Sunday evening will start me off much better on a Monday morning than having to stop and try to remember what it was I was going to do.

Family conferences:
If you are working, it will almost certainly be necessary for your husband and family to do more to help around the house. Initially it will take them a little while to get accustomed to this, so you can expect all the usual grumbles and mutterings to take place!

Many women (myself included) usually cave in at this point, feeling guilty that they have not been able to do everything themselves as before. So they drag themselves around after an exhausting day, feeling more and more under pressure and less and less able to give their families the love and attention that is far more necessary than a spotless kitchen and an empty ironing basket.

We very easily fall into the trap of imagining that the most important thing is to keep the house looking spick and span rather than making the people in it feel loved and wanted. Time to listen to little Johnny's problem is far more important than time to clear up the front hall—especially when we get all uptight again if anyone dares to untidy it!

Children can actually enjoy helping out if they can feel that we honestly appreciate it and are prepared to leave them with the full responsibility of doing something for us, without breathing down their necks to see if they are doing it right. The first hurdle of getting them organized is always the worst!

Similarly, although a husband may know that his wife has been out working all day, and will appreciate the extra income that it brings in, he may still not have fully understood the implications of this—that she simply hasn't had time to finish ironing his shirts, that the supper is nowhere near ready when he comes home. Men are often unaware of what has to be done around the house. They imagine that when their wives are at home they usually have nothing to do all day or that, if they are working, it can all be done in half an hour with the minimum of effort and no help!

Open, honest communication with all the family about the new situation can prevent a lot of really stormy water ahead. Alas, so often it is so much easier to maintain a martyred silence and hope that someone will eventually realize, which of course they never do!

7. The Homemaker

I will never forget the year we returned from India to live in this country, moving into our new house shortly before Christmas. The place was freezing and we had nothing but garden chairs to sit on. With our two tiny children we struggled to try and feel that we belonged somewhere in this country. In the days that followed not one of the neighbours came over either to ask if we needed anything nor to invite us in. Eventually someone from the church did call to deliver the parish magazine, but any hopes of hospitality and friendship that lay in this direction were quickly dashed. She was very busy, and would tell the vicar about us at a later date!

I mention this only because it still typifies much that passes for hospitality in this country. There is a well-known joke overseas which says that, while the Englishman may possibly ask you to tea, the American will ask you to stay for a week. Sadly, it is only too true!

People were much more hospitable to us abroad than they were in England. Yet Christians have been given a direct command to open their homes and receive strangers within their gates.

Housekeeping or hospitality

What has gone wrong, and why are we so insular, so self-protective in our thinking?

Certainly, it seems as if we have substituted good housekeeping for good hospitality. A housewife is judged good if her floors are well polished, her cushions tidy and her sink immaculate—but, while these may indeed be very desirable virtues, I think we should ask whether they are really Christian ones. Since it takes time and energy to achieve this polished Paradise, the danger is that we will seek at all costs to preserve it against the invading dirt and disorder that comes with visitors! I'm afraid it sounds rather more like the sin of pride than good homemaking.

Someone remarked to me not long ago that I was an unusual kind of housewife because I had a really nice home but didn't mind people coming into it—as if the two thoughts were entirely incompatible! And I well remember the comment of a friend some years ago, when we first started having quite large groups of people in our home for Christian meetings—'Well, of course, Ann,' she said glancing sideways at the none-too-tidy kitchen table, 'I can see you don't mind about keeping your home nice.' And I was left with no doubt in my mind as to who was the virtuous one in her eyes!

As in so many areas of our life we have to ask who wrote the script—why are we so obsessed with tidiness and cleanliness as if they really are next to godliness? Of course it is hard for the wife whose mother was a perfect housekeeper to relax and learn to live with a bit of children's chaos and a feeling of 'home' around the place. The tidiness tape has often been so well recorded on to our minds that we don't even stop to think let alone examine it in terms of Christian priorities. This is also a problem for husbands with very young children around creating chaos wherever they go. If a man comes from a house where tidiness mattered terribly he will inevitably set out to put pressure on his wife to keep their house tidy.

And indeed if we were brought up to believe that anything but a perfectly tidy, polished house is a disgrace, then it must also figure that the ultimate horror would be other people actually coming in and *seeing* it in a mess! We feel as if we will only be acceptable to outsiders if the place is immaculate! But is that true or right in God's eyes?

The year after we returned from India, we seemed to have an unending stream of visitors staying in the house—in fact from May to October I think we only had three weeks without one family or another staying. Now that would have been fine if it were not for one thing—up until this time I had never really learnt to keep house on my own!

Without my wanting to I had got used to everything being done for me by the stream of servants that were provided out in India. Now that I had returned to England with two tiny children, I was entirely on my own without any experience of housekeeping worth the name and running what amounted to a small hotel to boot!

I struggled by somehow, but only by disappearing for hours into the kitchen in a frantic effort to produce meals that were 'up to standard' with precious little know-how and often with a cookbook in one hand and a whimpering child in the other! At all costs, I felt, these visitors must not be allowed to see how badly I did things or how little I knew about keeping house!

Then suddenly, after a couple of months of exhausting and unnecessary effort, which involved my hardly ever having a moment to spend with the visitors who had actually come to see *us* and not to see how well I kept house, I realized how ridiculous all this was. I had allowed my pride and my deep sense of inadequacy to blind me to the need to welcome people into our home and let them see things just as they were. All this effort to put on a good show might have given the illusion of a well-run tidy house with reasonable meals but there was no question of it being a home!

Nowadays I am probably still a very chaotic and rather untidy housekeeper, but I can at least rejoice that the many people who pass through the house nearly always comment on how much they feel at home there.

Having time for one another

Children in particular suffer when homemaking turns into housekeeping. When they are always being asked to tidy up and are always being made to feel that they are in the way or creating work, then there is not a home. Of course the tidying up does have to be done, but equally children need to have a place where they can be themselves and relax without feeling that constant nagging pressure surrounding them.

Often we get so wound up with all the things that need doing that we do not actually realize what we are communicating by our over-tense, nervous busyness. What comes across is that a clean and tidy house matters more than a happy and relaxed family! Martha was the worried, flapping housekeeper in the Bethany home that Jesus knew so well but it was

Mary who, in His own words, had 'chosen the better part'—that of being with Him, listening to Him and making Him feel welcome. And I believe that this was not only true because it was her Lord that she was listening to. We have to stop and listen to the people who come to us for help, to the child who needs our time and our attention, without all the time straining to get on with the next job.

Clearly, we have got to get through the work somehow, but we must also get our priorities right! May I suggest that if you are constantly tense and under pressure you should stop and ask yourself what you are really doing and why? A family discussion, which draws out of everyone what they really feel about home and about Mum's and Dad's part in this, can be really revealing—if also somewhat painful!

A vision for the home

I do not believe that any more valuable centre exists in the whole community than a welcoming Christian home. The sad thing is that so few people recognize this fact. But if you look at a normal Christian home on the parish map and then notice how many families round about have been drawn into the fellowship, I believe that this will speak for itself. People instinctively go to a loving Christian home for help and support.

As more women are going out to work, the full-time home-maker with a vision for the home is more and more desperately needed. In the post-Christian climate of today's world, our witness has to begin in our homes and in our neighbourhood or it will scarcely begin at all!

By 'vision for the home', I do not mean a vision for

simply sitting at home waiting for the family to return! As I said before, it really frightens me how few people in this country have any concept of genuine hospitality or of opening their homes for God and others to use. So, while we sit at home convinced that 'This is where God wants me to be', we have to be very honest with ourselves about what we are actually doing.

Very probably we have our close friends and relatives in for meals or to stay with us, but what about others in need around us—lonely old folk who have few people to care for them, widows, divorcees, children whose parents live abroad, new arrivals—the list is endless. Often we will have to go out and look for these people praying that God will lead us to those who are right for us. Then we have to show genuine, wholehearted love for our neighbours—no strings attached.

The other day I met a woman whose caring vision had literally transformed her neighbourhood. After the death of her first husband from cancer, she did not sit at home feeling sorry for herself, but instead she went out into the area looking for people who needed her love and help. Now she has so many friends who look forward to her visits and find their way to her front door that God has given her a completely new family.

Just think what would happen if ever a few people caught this vision of genuine home-making in the area in which they lived!

Some Christians are so involved in church life and busyness, that, what with the PCC, the Bible Study Group, not to mention the flower rota or the church drains, they do not leave themselves enough time even to get to know their neighbours, let alone ask them round. When we had a church mission recently, it was shattering to hear some people say things like, 'Oh, we don't really know anyone outside to ask.'

Unfortunately what has now become known as the ghetto mentality affects most Christians in one way or another. Gradually as the years go by our friends get narrowed down to those who belong only to the Christian world. This not only limits the effective witness of our homes, it also prevents us from hearing the needs and the questions of people who never darken the doors of our churches. While we are patting ourselves on the back for our Christian involvement, we are actually losing touch with the very people we should be reaching!

When we realized that this creeping paralysis was beginning to affect our home as well, we put an instant stop to it. No more of our friends were to be asked to another meeting unless we had recently had them round for a meal or a drink because we cared about them and wanted to see them. First things first!

A house or a home

To define the difference between a house and a home is not easy but I asked my children to help me. Top of their priority list was the need for the house to look and feel lived in with a bit of healthy muddle around the place. People who come and go should be treated as part of the family without any special ceremony being put on for them, which they always find embarrassing and difficult to cope with when they go to visit friends.

Warmth and colour are an essential ingredient. Often Christians are so guilt-ridden about spending money on making their homes look and feel welcoming, that the necessary extra touches of colour and character provided by pictures, cushions, plants and a few really comfortable chairs, are somehow lacking.

Children should be free to come and go unless the adults have something special on or it is past bedtime. The more people we have passing through our homes, the greater the mutual benefit provided that we can relax and carry on normally. Certainly our children now have little or no problem meeting and talking with adults. Their lives have also been greatly enriched by the number and variety of people they know from all round the world, and above all by the genuine Christian testimony of people who have stayed in our home.

Over the years we have had several people living with us for an extended period of time. One girl was with us for almost five years. These people have very naturally become part of the family and again are a very enriching experience for all of us.

Lastly, though much higher up on the children's list, is the somewhat controversial question of having animals around the place. For us, and for our fellow countrymen, a house is not a home without animals but, of course, to others who were brought up without them, animals are dirty, noisy and unnecessary! There are obviously times when they are not an asset to have around—a cat who appears like magic the minute lunch is on the table or the dog who sticks a cold wet nose into people's faces during the prayer meeting. But personally I feel that animals are very much a part of family life—not least because so many English people find them so much easier to relate to than people! Few of our visitors have escaped being presented with the rabbit or the guinea-pig to cuddle at some point—and fewer still seem to have minded in the least!

Of course, it is not possible to lay down the ideal blueprint for someone else's home, but if we understand the love of God and His command to be salt and light in the community around us, we have to learn to be home-makers for Him, whether we are married or single, working outside or at home, rich or poor. Our homes will show what He is really like.

8. The Single Woman

While I was still unmarried at the ripe old age of twenty-six, I remember thinking that I was never going to meet the man who was right for me. After the death of a boyfriend while I was at university, it seemed that no one else I met would ever fill that gap and, after a fairly traumatic and unhappy childhood, this felt like God's ultimate rejection of me as a person. He might love others around me but I was clearly not included!

I remember a friend telling me one day that God loved each one of us so much that He could really be trusted to provide exactly what we needed. At the time I thought rather cynically that I would believe it when I saw it—but that was indeed exactly what happened for me only a few months later. I do not think that it was any coincidence that it happened after I had wholeheartedly given the future to God, no strings attached.

Do we really want what God wants for us, whatever that may include, or are we holding out on Him? Is there a qualifying clause in the margin of our minds?

The trouble is that, as time goes on and our other friends get married, the pressure from all sides intensifies, so that our minds become filled with this one single thought—how and where we may meet the man of our dreams. And though we may begin by trusting God with this problem it is very tempting to snatch it back again from Him and start putting our own 'Plan B' into operation—try a different church, engineer another meeting with someone who is not a Christian, and so on!

Over the last few years, I have been alongside a number of single girls in their twenties and thirties....

Rachel had just left university and was quite a character. After a fairly unhappy childhood, she was desperate to get married quickly and tested every man she met with this in mind. Knowing that she had a great many problems to work through before she would even begin to *recognize* the right man for her, let alone be ready to settle down in marriage, I tentatively suggested that she might well not get married before her late twenties. The horror and disbelief on her face said it all, and she continued to look around hopefully at all comers!

As the years went by, Rachel changed and grew both in her own personal faith and in her own identity. She came to know God's love for her and to realize her own value as a person. The change that took place in those few years was little short of total. From an unhappy angry sort of girl, she developed into someone with humour and compassion and a great love for God that led her into full-time Christian service. Then, as so often happens, she eventually met the man who was right for her while she was wholeheartedly involved with her work for God and not even thinking about marriage! What is more, the man she married was completely different from the men she was originally attracted to—relationships which at the time, as I knew only too well, would have ended in total disaster! God in his love knew that she had to change and grow as a person before she could marry the man God had chosen for her.

One of the biggest single causes of marriage break-up today is that of girls marrying too young before they have reached maturity or found their own settled identity. Unfortunately this is true for Christians also—indeed, perhaps even more true!

Firstly, there is the rather naive belief that if the man who says he loves me is a Christian, then this relationship must be right and of the Lord! Secondly, to compound the problem, there is the unhappy fact that there are still more Christian women than men around, thus limiting the choice even further. How vital, then, to be really sure that marriage is God's plan for us and not something that we have engineered, out of a determination to be married at all costs.

From my years of counselling, I can tell you that to be unhappily married because we have tied ourselves down to the wrong man is far worse than to be single. And we have to beware of the Enemy tempting us to believe otherwise. Genesis 3 verse 16, where God tells us that our desire shall be for our husband and he shall rule over us, should warn us about this.

We have to believe that God's infinite wisdom and love knows what is right and good for us. Whether this means waiting longer to get married or whether it means remaining single, we must trust Him whole-heartedly with the future and take our minds off what can so easily become an all-pervading obsession!

Pam is now in her early thirties and each year she is growing more fulfilled and happy in her single existence. The middle child in a family where she was constantly criticized and repressed, it has taken her quite a long time to find her own identity. Until very recently, she believed that the only reason she was on this earth was to do her duty and meet the needs of other people. She was at everyone's beck and call, far above and beyond the demands that God was actually making on her—and it was not a joyful giving of herself either.

Over the years more than one man had proposed marriage but, although they were Christians, she was aware that they looked on her as someone to lean on—they wanted a mother and not a wife. Happily for Pam she knew at first-hand from her own family, how bad a marriage on this basis could be and, despite the pressures, God has helped her to stand out against it.

The secret of her freedom has been a discovery of God's great love and concern for her as an *individual in her own right*. She knows now that He loves her and has chosen her and that she has a real value in being herself, whether or not she ever marries. In the beginning this came about through the care and concern of one family, who gave her the love she had never had as a child. Then subsequently she experienced it through a counselling group, where the other members helped her to see herself through their eyes and now finally she knows God's love for her in a far-seeing church, which provides for its single people without making them feel second-class citizens.

A very large part of the problem for single people is that no one makes a place for them in the ordinary run-of-the-mill activities, whether it be in the church or in their social life. If they are included at all—and too often they are forgotten or left out—it is only to make up the numbers. Or they are lumped in with other married folk all the time, which only underlines the problem for them.

Effectively, we are saying to them, 'There is only room for you if you are married like everyone else.' When this is very often the deepest desire of their own hearts, this is surely a doubly cruel blow.

Single people need somewhere to belong and a fellowship and social life of their own. We have married groups, and young people's groups but suddenly, after a certain age, it all dries up and there is often nowhere for the single person to go where they can find the fellowship and support that we all so badly need.

Some twenty-five years ago, a handful of Christian men, working in London, started a small group for other professional people in need of fellowship. Together with their girl-friends they met together both for Bible-study, supper parties and normal social activities and the idea spread like wildfire. In just a few years, the number of groups became so large that they had to appoint their own chaplain and counsellor. Through this fellowship, large numbers of single Christians met and married each other and started a vital grape-vine of support for both singles and marrieds that stretched the length and breadth of the country, including the children who are now rapidly growing up.

This group has now officially ceased to exist, because it was thought better that people should find their fellowship in the local church—but personally, I wonder. It seems to me that we need more rather than fewer groups like this. How else are Christian single people to find fellowship and a sense of well-being in today's world if they do not happen to come from a church where there are plenty of others of their own kind? The temptation must inevitably be to move out and thus fall into the arms of others who would eagerly receive them—and the fall-out rate among Christian girls for this reason remains alarmingly high.

Of course, it is true that if God plans for people to meet and marry they will do so, and it is equally true that our lives should be centred on Him, seeking first His kingdom, and all these things will be added unto us, but single people have to survive in everyday life like the rest of us. They need the love, the friendship and the fellowship of others in the same position without feeling that they are the odd one out with nowhere to go.

The single career girl

Girls who continue their early careers on into their late twenties and early thirties without marrying are almost bound, if they have any ability, to get quite high up on the ladder of success. Surely we should rejoice that there are quite a number of gifted Christian women doing very well in jobs that matter right across the spectrum of society.

Susan Marchant is a twenty-nine year old career girl, happily occupied running a busy office for a small firm of architects. She loves her work and the responsibility that goes with it and she enjoys being a woman in a business world. Her father always encouraged her to do well at school and to make the best of herself and her opportunities and she does just that. But recently, the outside pressures in her life have become almost intolerable. Both her parents are constantly asking her when she's going to get married—even though they know perfectly well that there is no one on the horizon after a recently broken engagement. Most of her Christian friends are already married and she is finding the church fellowship where she goes harder and harder to cope with. When she is at work she has the respect and friendship of the men she works with, but in the church the situation is very different—successful single women clearly have no part in their type-casting! The Bible-study group is run by a man who is not a natural leader and has very little idea of what constitutes a good group meeting. Although she would love to help, it is made quite clear that this is not 'a woman's role' within the church. So gradually Susan is being driven further and further away from the two supports that she most badly needs—her home and her church—towards people in the outside world, many of them married already, who enjoy her company and give her a real sense of value and belonging.

The problem is that there are many people in our churches who feel that there is somehow something wrong with successful single women and so make no provision for them within the church structures. It seems that women like Susan are expected to shed their abilities at the church door and play what the church considers 'a woman's role'—whatever that might be!

We will look at this issue in greater detail in the chapter on women in the church, but it is a very particular problem for single professional women. Outside the church they are valued as people in their own right, but inside they find themselves rejected and devalued. Add this to the burden of belonging to a church where most other people are married and we can see why single girls feel alienated and almost driven out to find friendship and support elsewhere—and not necessarily in the most helpful quarters either!

The value of singleness

A woman without family ties has more freedom than married women to serve God and to find herself as the kind of person He wants her to be. St Paul in 1 Corinthians 7 advises his single readers that it is better to stay unmarried if possible. Again in verse 34 he says that 'a girl who is not married is anxious to please the Lord in all that she is and does. But a married woman must consider other things such as housekeeping and the likes and dislikes of her husband.' A single woman can give her time to God and to others to a degree which no married woman with a family could begin to consider. How vital then that a single woman should pray that she will be given a real vision for this and for the way ahead to open up for her.

Too often in the past singleness has been seen as some terrible negative burden for a woman to carry. In the bad old days, when society demanded that a woman should be married, a single woman became a companion or a governess. There was really nothing else that she could do to make her way in the world. At least today, although things can still be tougher for a woman than a man, we have the freedom to take up whatever career we feel called to and to use some, if not all, the gifts that God has given us.

Providing that she has a loving, supportive fellowship, life has much greater potential for the single girl in the twentieth century than it has ever had at any other time down the ages. Sadly, though, this is not the case if she wishes to pursue a career in the church!

What, then, are the problems for a single career girl? Without doubt one of these will emerge from the non-Christian sidelines. While so many marriages are breaking up in the world around her, and others outside the church now have what they like to call a 'liberated attitude to sex', an attractive, unattached woman becomes a target for all comers. Add to this the fact that she may well long to be married, and you have a ready-made problem almost constantly waiting in the wings for the single girl!

How vital then that she should have a group of Christian friends with whom she can identify and where she can feel she really belongs—a bolt-hole from the temptations that will very likely assail her at regular intervals.

It is equally vital that this fellowship should be a place where she can talk about her needs and her feelings openly, without having to cloak them under a veil of superficial spiritual language. So often single girls at this stage in their lives have few, if any, other unmarried friends left to talk to and the need for open, honest communication, where poeple can help and encourage one another has become even more essential.

Another problem for the single girl is the down-to-earth, practical business of trying to run a flat or a house on her own. It is not just a matter of starting work all over again with the washing and the cooking the moment she returns home from work, but it is also the financial burden, the worry of managing single-handed, and having to cope with the simple little jobs like putting up shelves and clearing out the drains that a man around the house would normally do.

How lovely it would be if the family of God were really operating as He planned that it should—if we actually loved one another enough within the fellowship to see each other's needs and to come alongside to help without having to be asked.

Who am I?

Just as the insecure married woman may feel that her only value lies in being someone's wife, equally the single woman may feel that she has no value because she is not! Both feelings may reflect unhelpful attitudes prevalent in society but they are categorically not what Scripture teaches. Each one of us has a great value in our Master's eyes and His love will reach to the ends of the earth to watch over and care for us.

So often Christians do not fully understand this teaching. They speak of individuals as 'channels' only, 'vessels for His use' and so on. Certainly we can find this teaching in Scripture but it is not intended to knock the already insecure and unloved person further into the ground and there are plenty of other verses to balance this out. In Isaiah 49 it tells us that He cares about us so much that 'we are graven on the palms of His hands'. And Matthew 10 verse 30 says that 'even the very hairs of our head are numbered'. We did not choose Him, but He chose us!

If we have not found our own identity in God's eyes and in our own understanding, the waters of life will continue to be pretty choppy ahead! A great many problems for both married and single people are caused by this single factor—that they have not found their identity and do not know their own worth.

When this is a problem for the married woman she at least has the love of her husband and children to support her. For the single woman the scene is very different. It is often the single woman who has not known the love and affirmation of accepting parents. Now her unmarried state feels like final confirmation that she is unwanted and unworthy of anyone's love. The problems may have started way back in childhood, very often with an unloving or unhelpful father/daughter relationship. A father's love is supposed to provide a pattern for relating to someone of the opposite sex and many a father has a lot to answer for in the way he has failed his daughter in this area.

This may even be the reason why the single woman has never married. A feeling of being unloved and rejected transmits itself through everything we do so that someone with this kind of background is often almost apologizing for being alive. The invisible bubble over her head actually spells out, 'Don't look at me, I'm not worth getting to know'. If she has not found a career to give her a sense of value, then the single woman has nothing to make her feel her own worth in the world.

It is easy for Christians outside this situation to glibly spiritualize it, saying things like, 'Well, surely the love of God is sufficient?' But actually, true as this may ideally be, it is not enough. I am sure that Jesus, who commands us to love one another as He has loved us, is aware of this fact. We are to provide love and encouragement for one another within the fellowship—and this is especially true for single people, widows and orphans who have no one else to support and affirm them. It needs other people to show, in the name of Christ, the reality of God's love in the everyday walk of life.

The Christian girl has a loving Heavenly Father to erase and re-write the harmful memories but they do have to be brought to Him for healing and not be hidden away from view. And she will not bring them to Him if she feels He will reject her.

If a single woman is able positively to see her worth as an individual in her own right, and to know deep within her how much God loves her, then she will be able to live a life of real fulfilment in the world.

9. The Widow and the Divorcee

If life is sometimes difficult for the single woman, it is impossible to compare it with the problems of the widow or the divorcee—and maybe this is why there is so much concern in the New Testament for the cause of widows in the church.

One widow said to me recently: 'A lot of people seem to have the mistaken idea that after six months or so the pain diminishes, but actually the alone-ness and the sense of only being half a person has never really gone. Once you have been happily married, it is so hard to get used to being alone again and to the lack of masculine company.'

In common with many others, this lady found the help and understanding of some Christians to be sadly lacking when her husband died. Another young widow I know found fellow Christians in her church so hurtful and unhelpful that she could not bring herself to stay in the area.

All Yvonne needed was a shoulder to cry on and some loving on-going support but the experience was clearly too painful for her fellow-Christians to cope with. Some came and tried to cheer her up, saying that God must have some clear purpose in what had happened. Others came for a while, leaving her another 'good' book to read, and a great many more stayed away, unable to face up to the pain that she was feeling. Yvonne lost not only her husband but also her faith because no one was prepared to stay with her in the pain. They could not bear to hear the bad things she was feeling—the hurt, the anger and the impossible grief.

Why does this happen and why do we find it so hard to face other people's suffering? One reason I am sure is that as Christians we feel we ought to have 'an answer'—a neat little text we can hand someone to wrap up the problem and put it safely away.

But is this what Jesus did? At the tomb of Lazarus he wept. He was known as a 'man of sorrows, acquainted with grief'. We live in a fallen world and there are no easy answers for the pain and problems that surround us on every side—uncomfortable as some people may find this to be!

Facing up to our own pain

Another problem about helping people who are suffering bereavement is that it may well stir up memories of hurts that we have not come to terms with in ourselves. When my neighbour's husband was killed in a plane crash a few years back, I found it incredibly hard to face her grief. My feet were like lead as I walked down the road to see her. Hearing her pain had stirred up in me memories of bereavements in my own life that I had never dealt with and never cried over.

Some years later, now I have faced up to the pain hidden in the basement of my own life and cried for the many bereavements I had experienced, I find myself infinitely more able to be alongside those suffering in this way—without the neurotic need to 'say something Christian', in order to fill the silence or make me feel better. The true love of Christ in these situations is to be alongside and to bear the pain, and to speak only when we are really certain of what God is saying to us.

Sadly, a great deal in our British culture militates against this. We are often brought up to hide our feelings and maintain a 'stiff upper lip' in all circumstances! Very likely we will despise and reject the overt emotional weeping and wailing that goes on in Southern Europe and the Arab countries. However, if we swallow our pain and push it out of sight we are denying ourselves the God-given means of healing that comes with tears and a verbal expression of the pain within.

The need to talk about it

One widow said to me that on the day her husband died it was almost as if he had never existed—no one wanted to talk about him and no one could listen without embarrassment to the memories she wanted to share. When her many friends, who could have helped her keep his memory alive, refused to do so because of their own anxieties, her sense of loss became all the more acute.

When Yvonne came to see us, after being unable to talk to anyone for so long about the wonderful husband she had lost, the memories simply poured out of her in an almost uncontrollable stream. But, as she spoke, her face began to lighten and you could see that she was re-experiencing living with him and even beginning to see that God had taken him and that He was still 'there'. As her pain and her memories were accepted in the name of Christ, she showed in her eyes the hope of returning faith.

Of course, allowing a woman to talk about memories of her dead husband and of the feelings that are going on inside of her is never a safe and easy passage—which may be one very good reason why so many people are afraid to face this.

Sometimes she will talk of fantasies that he is coming back, and the listener feels that these should be corrected or denied. Of course the widow herself knows deep down that they are not true. The creation of a dream world where this terrible thing never happened is a kind of sub-conscious delaying tactic to avoid facing up to the inevitable. But as the weeks and months go by she will gradually be able to face up to the truth—more especially if she has the wonderful Christian assurance that she will see him again one day.

Listening may well involve us in hearing about the anger that a bereaved person sometimes feels against God, and this can be very uncomfortable indeed. We want to leap to God's defence and tell her she ought not to be feeling like this. But God does not need our defence; He who took our pain and grief on the Cross, has already accepted that anger. We too must accept it in the name of Christ, thus allowing her to free herself from her pain.

One of the clearest principles in the Bible is that God brings joy out of suffering, but understandably we would much rather not have the suffering in the first place! Over and over again, people have said that the bereavement, the imprisonment or the loss as brought them much closer to God. Perhaps initially the coming to God is reluctant, rising out of desperation, but He has promised to bind up our hurts and to make a way that we may be able to bear it.

God's forward planning

One widow in our parish has a lovely testimony of how God prepared her beforehand for what was going to happen. Some years before her husband's death, when the children were still quite young, she had a definite sense that God was calling her to teach. She had no particular desire to do this and not many academic qualifications either, but she went ahead with her training. So when her husband died Joyce was a fully qualified teacher, teaching at a primary school just a few hundred yards from her own front door.

Another of God's coincidences was that in her last year at College she had found herself doing a study on the Hebrew and Christian beliefs concerning life after death—something that helped her greatly at the time of her bereavement. She feels that many Christians would find it easier to come through such a crisis if they really knew the foundations of their faith and believed the promises of God.

Her husband's funeral stands out in many people's minds because, instead of disappearing quickly in the funeral car, Joyce stood at the back of the church and thanked those who came—a gesture that left many people amazed at her courage and strength.

Looking back now, Joyce finds it hard to believe that she was able to do this and then go on teaching as before without a break. Out of nowhere she was given a strength that was not her own and a deep sense of joy in the certainty that her husband was with Jesus.

Over the years since his death, Joyce has grown very remarkably as a Christian despite her aloneness and her many problems. She has become a lovely, radiant person who walks daily with God. Her children have grown up and left home and she is now head mistress at another school, where she leads a full life, being used by God in many different ways.

The divorcee

When a woman is widowed the tragic loss will rob her of a life-time companion but it cannot take away the knowledge of his love and the memory of the good times they once had together. For the divorcee it is very different. Little or nothing remains that she can believe in or hold on to. Most of what there was will have turned to ashes.

Even if the early years of the marriage were good, the memory of them will now be coloured by the bitter memories that followed—indeed, by mistrust of the reality of that love in the first place. Even the children are a constant reminder of what is now lost. Sometimes they will look and sound so like their father that this in itself becomes a further source of pain.

And finally, to add ultimate mockery to the situation, some Christians are so judgmental and unaccepting of her and her former husband because they are 'divorced' that even the church appears to have turned its back on them. Then there is that awful unspoken implication that they must somehow be to blame for the situation or they could surely somehow get back together again.

This is neither the time nor the place to talk about the rights and wrongs of divorce itself, but as one in three marriages inside and outside the church are breaking up, so one third of the families in this country are having to face the pain and loneliness of a separated life-style: an ex-wife wondering if her husband ever loved her in the first place, enduring the knowledge that her marriage has been a failure, suffering from a sense of total rejection and unhappy, confused children usually totally dependent on their mother for fathering and mothering at a time when she feels least able to give this.

The burdens now placed on the shoulders of the divorced woman are enormous. Often she will have had to move to a smaller house—if she has been lucky enough to find anywhere. Finance will be a much greater burden and she will have to try and get a job to help support the children. Once she is home in the evening, in addition to the housework there are the needs of the children, far greater and more pressing than they ever were before.

Children suffer much more in a divorce situation than is ever realized for they experience it as a personal rejection of themselves. 'How could my father possibly leave me if he really loved me?' is the constantly reiterated cry. Moreover, any visits to or from the absent parent are bound to stir up bitterness and resentment which will spill over on to the children. For a child it can be a situation fraught with tension and unhappiness, in which he simply cannot win.

How the church family can help

Within the church family we can help to alleviate the pain of widows and divorcees and their children if we include them lovingly and naturally in the activities of our own families.

A woman who loses her husband loses a great many other things on top of this terrible bereavement. She is alone, missing desperately the companionship, care and love she once had, yet just at this time, just when she most needs friendship, the usual social avenues are blocked. As a married couple she and her husband were both welcome in most mixed gatherings but, alone, she has no normal access to such company. People might ask her from time to time to make up the numbers, but she is very conscious that this is a charitable gesture and she is the odd one out.

Often this kind of hospitality requires unselfishness on our part and honesty between husband and wife about some of the feelings they are experiencing.

Yvonne said to us that she was aware that many wives seemed to fear that she was 'after their husbands' when all she actually needed was the comfort of a bit of masculine company. True as this may be for most widows and divorcees, an element of sexual need and attraction can creep in.

The sudden deprivation of a husband's love and protection and the accompanying sexual frustration after years of married life will inevitably leave a hurt and damaged woman, much in need of consolation— often with a distinct orientation towards the opposite sex. Whilst it would be quite wrong to be afraid of this, or to allow it to get in the way of the loving hospitality we are called upon to give one another in Christ's name, it could be equally stupid to ignore this dimension.

1 Timothy 5 contains a lot of teaching on the subject of widows in society, and although Paul may seem to be hard on some of the widows that he speaks about, there could be a warning in this for us. It is

certainly true in society today that many marriages are being broken up by other women who, having been hurt in divorce or bereavement, are looking for consolation wherever they can find it.

Paul's thoughts at the beginning of 1 Timothy 5 should be a guide to all of us in this area. We are called to regard one another as brothers and sisters in the Lord—naturally, without embarrassment and with pure thoughts as well! When the husband and wife have a really good relationship, however, this problem seldom arises.

One divorcee returned to our parish as the only place where she and her husband had ever been happy together. Without judgement or criticism, Jane became part of the wider church family, loved and welcomed in a large number of homes around the parish and feeling that she really belonged.

Over the years she worked through the pain of her experience and eventually she met and married someone very different from her first husband who was able to give both her and her daughter the love and support that they so much needed. But Jane would be the first to admit that *none* of this would have happened if the church had not welcomed them and provided them with the family life they had lost.

10. A Woman's Ministry in the Life of the Church

When our church first had a lady church-warden and then a lay-worker, some expressed feelings of doubt and anxiety. How would it work? Did we want the change? All kinds of fears flitted through the minds of some of the men about the rights and wrongs of women being involved in this kind of ministry, and many of the women, myself included, wondered if we wouldn't rather continue with men in these jobs as before. In the event, the actuality proved such a blessing to our church life, enriching and widening the ministry, that today we scarcely even think about it!

After I first wrote an article on the whole question of a woman's role in church life, I quickly came to the conclusion that this was a highly emotive issue on which people's opinions were far more subjective than they themselves realized! Often they would seem to be arguing quite powerfully from certain prohibitive verses of Scripture about women not teaching or leading but actually, when I pressed them further, something else much more fundamental would emerge.

Their doctrinal views about women in the church

mirrored almost exactly their feelings about women in life generally. Many of the men had been brought up to believe that a woman's place was in the home, or were themselves threatened by the thought of women in any kind of leadership position, whilst not a few of the women admitted that they needed a 'father figure' around. Of course, there is nothing intrinsically wrong with these feelings; they probably form a very powerful part of our background experience. The wrong lies in attempting to take them as an adequate foundation when formulating a theology of women in the church. The only foundation stone we should have is the teaching of Scripture on a woman's role in the church.

As I said in the first chapter of this book, women were heavily involved in the ministry of the early church and this was all the more remarkable since at that time Jewish women were not even allowed to sit with the men in the body of the synagogue, let alone help or take part in any way. If there was ever a time or a reason to keep women away from involvement in the life of a young growing church it was surely then! Yet we find a substantial number of women actually involved in ministry.

In a fascinating paper entitled 'The Role of Women in Scripture', Michael Griffiths, Principal of London Bible College, lays out the extent of this involvement.

The Philippian church actually began with a women's prayer meeting. In the letter to the Philippians, chapter 4, Paul (who is so frequently quoted as prohibiting the involvement of women) speaks of Euodia and Syntyche as 'fellow-workers labouring side by side with me for the cause of the Gospel'. The analogy is that of athletes in the same team, so that, far from denigrating the ministry of women, Paul is actually regarding them as fellow team members. Similarly, when Paul is writing to the church in Rome, he concludes with a list of greetings to ten women and nineteen men actually involved in the ministry to the congregation there. Little is said of them but again they are referred to as 'labouring in the Lord', a technical phrase used particularly of Christian ministry. As Michael Griffiths points out: 'There would seem to be as many women as men, perhaps even more, that are commended by Paul for their ministry. It is difficult to see how to harmonize this with the interpretation of Paul's words in other places, which would not allow women any significant ministry at all.'

Phoebe is spoken of as *diaconos* denoting the definite role of an officer of the church, and she is also referred to as *prostatis* which is taken from the verb meaning to stand in front or lead. Similarly, although the women in 1 Timothy 3 verse 11 are usually translated as 'deacons' wives', they were almost certainly female deacons. There is, Michael Griffithis says, no possessive pronoun in any of the manuscripts which would indicate that these were wives of the male deacons. Moreover, he points out that if 'deacons' wives' were really intended it is difficult to see why the bishop's wife should escape some honourable mention!

Also in Titus 2 verses 3–5 the older women are instructed to be *kalodidaskalous*, or, in other words, to be engaged in a teaching ministry. Some might say that this was, of course, to teach other women only, but Priscilla and Aquila were *both* engaged in teaching Apollos 'a more excellent way'. 2 Timothy 2 instructs that the Gospel is to be entrusted to faithful 'persons' (not men only) who will be able to 'teach others also' and, of course, Timothy himself received all his teaching from his mother and his grandmother. 'If,' says Michael Griffiths with tongue in cheek, 'women were really so gullible and unreliable and unfit to teach others, one questions whether Timothy's foundation would be as good as Paul says it is!'

Another favourite argument against the involvement of women in church leadership is based on the teaching about the voluntary submission of a wife to her husband. It is said that one may deduce from this that all women should be subject to all men. But this teaching is intended only for individuals within the marriage bond. Similarly, the fact that Genesis pictures a woman as a helpmeet for her husband does not indicate, as is so often assumed, that the woman is therefore inferior. For example, it is the greater (God) who helps the weaker (his people on earth). Or again, the use of the word 'head' to denote male superiority has the actual meaning of source or origin rather than leader or master, referring back to the creation story of the rib in Genesis.

The two or three negative Pauline passages about the ministry of women have been used with such heavy emphasis that it is difficult to deal with them with any kind of helpful balance.

Rather than take up the cudgels over these other passages as so many have attempted to do, let us start from this principle—if Scripture is to be seen as a united truth, which cannot contradict itself, Paul cannot in one place forbid the leadership or teaching of women and in another chapter openly commend women who are doing exactly this!

Whatever the other passages may teach, and let us leave the details to scholars and theologians, they cannot possibly mean what chauvinists in the church would have us believe. 1 Corinthians 14, where the women are commanded to keep silent in church, very probably refers to some particular problem in the Corinthian church. Perhaps the women were prophesying out loud, or questioning their husbands too much in public worship.

In 1 Timothy 2 verse 18 the women are instructed to learn in silence—which was, in those days, considered a sign of good breeding—and not to domineer over their menfolk, particularly their husbands. The force of the verb means to have full authority or power over men. Women are not to usurp authority and attempt to rule the roost.

In 1 Corinthians 11 Paul lays down the conditions under which a woman can pray or prophesy in public. She can only minister in this way when her head is covered. This was necessary in those days for women with uncovered heads were recognized as prostitutes.

Women in the church today

Until very recently women have played only a tiny part in the ministry of the church, busying themselves in cleaning the brass, arranging the flowers and keeping down the dust where the woodworm has got to the pews. Few people think like this any more, but many are unhappy about what a woman's role in the church really should be.

At the time of writing the Church of England still rules out the ordination of women, while openly admitting that it sees no obvious reason why this should not eventually come to pass! Meanwhile many churches in the Anglican Communion round the world have already taken this step. The Anglo-Catholics and the Roman Catholic Church itself utterly rule out any possibility of women priests, but some of the free churches have ordained women for many years now. At the same time some members of the house church movement are busy moving fast backwards into the dark ages where women have to keep silent and even wear quaint little head coverings!

Anxiety over the subject runs high and it is difficult to find anyone who is totally neutral. Some fear that women wardens or ministers will drive the men away, while others are unhappy with women in a role that they have been accustomed to men filling for years. Objections run from the bizarre to the very down-to-earth. One man actually said to me that a woman reading the lesson or taking the service might arouse undesirable sexual thoughts in his mind—and I honestly wondered if he thought that women were exempt from such feelings! Others concern themselves only with what a woman priest should wear, and I must admit that a dog-collar does not greatly enhance a woman's appearance!

Personally I have no very strong thoughts on the subject one way or the other, but I have two anxieties about the situation remaining as it is.

First, it does seem that God is calling out a number of extremely able women into the ministry at the moment and many are having to be turned away. Is it likely that so many gifted women would feel drawn to full-time commitment in His service if He did not actually want to use them? Surely we need all the gifted able ministers we can find to work for His Kingdom here on earth—and not only the men.

Secondly, the present situation, where a woman in the Church of England may become a deaconess but not a priest, take a service but not consecrate the Sacraments, and, whilst technically included as a member of Church staff, still be ranked as 'laity', seems a very unsatisfactory and almost dishonest compromise!

If God created men and women in His own image to stand side by side representing His nature, then is it really right to have just man representing Him? Should we not look for a partnership of some kind?

Sadly, so much of our thinking in this area is clouded and subjective. People seem to envisage a monstrous regiment of women, all made in the image of well-known feminists, overtaking the church like a flood. And anxiety fed by these frantic imaginings runs very high indeed! But those of us who have benefited from the ministry of loving, balanced God-fearing women can only see how much the church is losing out by this rather narrow, one-sided interpret-ation of Scripture. If God created us male and female in His image, then surely we need *both* to represent His church.

A woman can bring into the ministry of the church the full richness of God's creative purposes, her own feminine gifts complementing those of her masculine partners on the staff. For example, the church badly needs a woman's gentleness and understanding in its pastoral ministry because, although many men may be good at this, a woman brings something extra, simply through her natural femininity.

The constant preoccupation with whether a woman should or should not be allowed to take up leadership roles within the church has caused us to completely miss the point about leadership. Surely the only important criteria is whether or not a woman has the spiritual standing and necessary talent to do the job.

Can it really be God's will, as sadly sometimes

happens, for *any* man to lead the study group rather than a woman who is plainly more able? Can it be right for a woman to be held back from the ministry to which she feels called and for which she is clearly very qualified, simply because she is a woman? With prophets like Miriam and Deborah in the Old Testament, and with so many women involved in the ministry of the early church, we have surely to be very careful before we reject the whole idea of woman's ministry on the grounds of these three short contradictory passages in the writings of Paul.

11. The Creative Woman

The minute anyone uses a word like 'creative' in connection with womankind, the image of a slightly chaotic lady with long red hair dabbing away at an easel, throwing lumps of clay, or manufacturing dozens of neatly ruched lampshades immediately springs to our minds! But this aspect of a woman's creativity is only one very small corner of what I want to talk about.

To tell a woman that she must be creative in this way, when she knows she is not, only adds frustration and a further sense of guilt! The canvas of a truly creative woman stretches right across her world, bringing not only an artistic touch but also warmth, colour and understanding where there was often little or none before.

A friend recently described creativity as having three separate aspects. Firstly, there is the 'out of nothing' creativity that has to express itself in something like writing, painting or music and where the owner of that gift can only find herself as she uses this gift in some way. For example, since I was a tiny child I have needed to write—the results may not have been particularly brilliant and indeed at the ripe old age of ten I ceremonially burned a whole book of 'poetry' because, to my then superior judgement, it was 'so impossibly juvenile'! There is a creative urge in me that needs to be expressed on paper, and if I cannot find the time to get away and write, then I feel frustrated and restricted in my inner self. People who enjoy playing the piano, making things with their hands or dancing will very likely have experienced the same kind of urge or frustration. I believe that it is a God-given part of our nature that we deny at our peril.

Then there is creativity using available resources —and by that I do not just mean painting up jam-jars to look pretty or making useless knick-knacks out of loo rolls! This is a form of creativity which any woman can and should use in her everyday life.

A friend of ours can move into any situation and give her surroundings a feeling of life, colour and zest, using ways that none of us would have thought of. This summer when asked to make the children feel welcome on arrival at a school houseparty, she went straight out to erect a flotilla of balloons on the school gates and a frozen sack of ice lollies by the door. Show her a barren school dormitory or a chilly church hall and she will immediately set to work to transform it into something infinitely more welcoming and cheery, using a minimum of money and resources.

Sadly, it is this kind of creativity that I often find lacking in Christian homes and conference centres. Perhaps it stems from some kind of guilt complex about having to 'make do' with only the basics and a kind of pseudo-Spartan living, which we imagine is glorifying to God and edifying to the soul. But there is a world of difference between the obviously extravagant surroundings of those who leave God out of their thinking and the creation of a warm and colourful welcoming atmosphere with very little expenditure. Having lived in a condemned bungalow full of rats during the first few years of our married life in India, I do have some experience of what can be done with very little!

It is often the little touches of colour and attention to creative detail which actually do not cost a great deal that can bring the most dreary surroundings to life: posters on the wall, plants on the table or a few patches of bright colour to give lift to dreary rooms.

Look at almost any office or flat occupied by men only and it is very often barren, colourless and purely functional. Recently I observed one such office after a woman had moved in as well—in only a few weeks it had sprouted hanging plants, pictures on the wall and a complete re-arrangement of furniture resulting in a much more comfortable layout. Doubtless the men complained volubly about this female creative urge, but the transformation was remarkable!

And finally there is an aspect of creativity that many people have never even considered but which, to me, is one of the most important of all—that is creativity in relationships. Another friend of mine springs immediately to mind. Sally is a very busy career woman, and unless you knew her well you would never know the creativity she displays—it is all achieved quietly and unobtrusively in one-to-one encounters. Put her down in any conference or social gathering and she will have drawn out the shyest person and made them feel welcome and important. If there was someone in trouble or with a family in need, she would be hot on the scent, not just in casual sympathy but in order to lead that person on to someone who can really help. When people are with her they feel immediately aware of their value in her eyes and of their own sense of worth. This kind of creativity is truly like gold-dust.

I do not believe that there is any woman reading this whose creative gifts do not fall into one of these categories and maybe, in some way, into all of them. The problem is so often to recognize these gifts and then to give ourselves both the permission and the outlets to put them to work.

Guilt feelings

Unhappily, Christians generally strike me as very unproductive. They are full of guilt about their creativity. Often our whole lives get so narrowed down into a single-minded pursuit of what is overtly 'Christian' and recognizably 'fruitful' that we miss out on a great many of the creative possibilities around us. In consequence, the light of God that is allowed to shine through us is reduced to only a narrow and none too attractive flicker, instead of the full richness of the stained-glass window that God planned when He created us.

One of the barriers that kept me away for many years from wanting to be involved with Christian people was the narrow colourless image that so many of them displayed to the outside world. I saw it in the way they walked, the way they dressed and the way they seemed to be blinkered to the great potential that God had given them. Happily I then met others who could show me much more of His creativity— but let this be a wholesome reminder to those of us who are afraid to move forward in this area!

Often, our creative instincts are so well buried beneath a heap of 'oughts' and fears that we do not even know what it is we want to do, anyway. There is just a vague, distant longing for something that will make our lives richer and more varied, for another way to express ourselves. If this is the case, then a simple prayer that God will unlock the door and enable us to see the other riches we possess, will often show us in which direction to go. Perhaps, a close friend who is more aware of our gifts than we ourselves are may advise us.

Over the last year alone, I have watched as one friend after another has begun to discover new creative abilities and possibilities. One has suddenly had the urge to start playing the clarinet, another has blossomed in the realization that her great gifts lie in building and making relationships, and still another has discovered the joy of learning to dance and move her body, unlocking all the fears and inhibitions that have held her back for so long.

Time

Often time is at such a premium in our lives that to spend it on something as seemingly 'useless' as attempting to draw a picture or to play the piano for half an hour can make us feel riddled with guilt. When I saw the piano open with some incredibly complicated music at a friend's house the other day, she very quickly found it necessary to justify herself by saying that it kept her in practice for the teaching that she did. I just felt sad that she needed to justify spending time in this way.

When the creativity of God is so very evident all around us, do we really need to stop and ask 'What use is a butterfly?' or 'Who will ever see the tiny flower that gets trodden underfoot by the roadside?'

Each and every thing of beauty in the heavens and on the earth shows us more about the incredible creativity of our God.

Another barrier to creativity is the fact that we do not allow ourselves time to 'take in' as well as to give out. Most of us will attempt, come what may, to spend time alone with God, reading His word and talking to Him, but how much time do we allow ourselves to enjoy the beauty in the countryside around us or to listen to a really lovely piece of music? Do we spend time with friends, simply because we enjoy their company and because they give to us in some way that we cannot really define? So often we run ourselves almost dry of colour and breadth in our lives in a frantic scramble to get on with the next thing. Is it any wonder that our creativity dries up?

They say....

Another factor that frequently gets in the way of true creativity is our concern with what other people will say. Will they think it is worth doing? Will they laugh at us or, worse still, will they heap on to us still more guilt feelings about the fact that 'the time could be better used'?

The same can be true of any change in the way we dress or improvements to the home. The unspoken accusation is, 'Well, how much did that cost then? Did you really need it?' But does God call us to such a totally spartan way of life that we must lose all sense of colour and warmth in the process? As in all things we need to preserve a balance between an awareness of other people's need and the enjoyment of some of the good things that He provides for our use.

Creativity in relationships

Very often people get stuck in this area of their lives because they do not know how to move on beyond the status quo. They know where they would like to get to, but candidly have no idea how to reach that point in reality. Love remains an impossible dream.

This may be true of our relationships with our husbands, our children or just the friends down the road. Sometimes we even work out what we would like to say to people but, when it comes to the point, sadly we never say the words.

A woman with a creative gift in relationships may need to be told about the incredible gift she has, because in general it has no recognizable price-tag attached! We live in a lonely world, in a country where valuing and affirming one another is not a normal activity, and so the ability to mix and make friends is at an all-time premium.

With a creative gift like this, the world is a woman's canvass. Of course, it must begin at home with the encouragement and affirmation of her husband and her children. But, beyond the front door, the opportunities are endless. However, just as a natural gift for art or music may need more training to help it to grow, so the gift of making relationships may benefit from a basic training in counselling.

Creativity with available resources

Over and above the colour and character of the homes we live in and the clothes we wear, comes another and in many ways more valuable creative gift—that of seeing what can be done in our parish, our neighbourhood or our surroundings.

Often I find ideas of this kind come to me in the middle of the night or when I am miles away on holiday. I suddenly see in a flash of unusual clear-sightedness something that needs to be done! Perhaps if a group of people with similar gifts or needs met together they might spark off something really good. Maybe they would see some work opportunity that they could undertake together. The woman in Proverbs saw a field and bought it to plant a vineyard; she saw the needs of the poor around her and got on and did something about it! Do we perhaps see the need but then find that time shuts it out and we do nothing with the ideas that God has given us?

12. The Way Ahead

The work that occupies us for so many hours each day has been so devalued in the eyes of the world, that we have a deep-felt longing that someone will wake up and realize this and give us back some recognition and respect! I am sure it is no accident that so many articles have appeared in recent years listing all the different chores a woman performs in a single day, with an estimated wage-packet for each one, whether it be cook or laundress, driver or mender, nanny or shopper! This is one way of saying that we need to know what we are worth in the world.

Ironically the derogatory attitude adopted to women and to housework, has boomeranged to damage those very people who, by demeaning women, are seeking to protect themselves. George Gilder, in a book entitled *Sexual Suicide*, puts forward this view. His theory is that, while the ability to have children confirms womanhood and ensures all (or most?) women a useful role in society, men have no such utilitarian value, unless their role as bread-winner and head of the family is granted to them. In the meantime, he says, women have entered the career world for two main reasons. Natural skills, such as homemaking, have been devalued in a world that sees academic ability as the only skill of any worth. In addition to this, housework is not remunerated and of course everything in today's world is valued according to its commercial worth. Many husbands, he says, have been guilty of reflecting the world of commerce in this respect, making the housewife feel that she is not doing anything of real value. On this theory any husband who despises his wife for possessing only housewifely skills is acting suicidally because inevitably she will seek her worth outside the home, thereby reducing his own sense of worth.

George Gilder is certainly speaking of values as they exist in the world today—values that we have all been brought up with. If he is right, then all our attitudes must change. Instead of going on endlessly about 'a woman's place' and 'submission' we must get society to affirm the value of women's work.

I believe we can do this within a Christian marriage where there is a deep concern for one another's welfare. If we are each looking to the other's needs, then we will be able to talk about our deeper longings and the ways in which we experience each other's support, or lack of it. If the wife is needed at home either for the sake of the children or to run the home, then she will certainly need all the love and affirmation that her husband can give her—and if he does not realize this then she must express it as clearly and lovingly as possible. Alas, it is always much easier to say accusingly, 'You never remember to show appreciation of anything that I do', than simply to say, 'Look, darling, I need to know that you appreciate what I am doing and not to feel you are just taking me for granted!' Communication at this level may take time to achieve and it is a question of perseverance.

We ourselves must make sure that we are clear in our own minds about the vital part we are playing in the life of the home and family entrusted to us. Often women can help one another with this understanding and with the realization that children are not around for ever, so that the years spent with them are very precious indeed.

But then we come to the question of whether or not a man *should* feel threatened if women seek careers outside the home. Understanding that this thought does exist in the minds of many men is, I believe, half the battle. I personally think that the 'sexual suicide' theory is a dated one, going back to the roles men have become accustomed to. All that is threatened is a social custom not man in nature.

If, for example, a woman with school-aged children feels the need to find something useful to do with her time, then how can a truly loving husband turn to her and say, 'Well, I need you *not* to do this, because I feel it devalues me'? True, they might begin at this point, for the sake of an open, honest discussion, but surely he will try to hear and understand her need, while she seeks to reassure him about his value and his status in her eyes and in the eyes of the world.

The real root of the trouble

I think we do well to understand that all such inter-sex rivalry is basically about insecurity and personal devaluation—and this is as true for the man as it is for the woman. A man who objects to career women is really only saying that they make him feel insecure and devalued—that they threaten his own identity and feeling of self-worth. And the reason for this will almost certainly be that he has been brought up to believe that it is a man's 'role' to be the breadwinner and a woman's 'role' to look after the home. We do well to remember this, meeting all such attitudes with loving Christian understanding rather than an aggressive resentment.

I am sure it is no coincidence that every single man who has spoken to me *positively* about how good it is to have women around in the business and committee world, has shown a positive self-image and awareness of his own identity and God's love for him.

It is interesting to see that, in the generation now growing up, a much more equal partnership is coming into being, where men expect women to work alongside them without even thinking of this in terms of a threat.

A career or a family—can I have it all?

But what of the successful single career woman who longs to get married and have children, but wonders if she can keep both careers? Is this possible and can we, as Christians, even see it as right?

It is never right to tell someone else how to live their lives, but two important facts have to be borne in mind here. There is very little that is worth having in God's world, without sacrifice. This is a basic principle of the Christian life as Jesus Himself showed us. Moreover, we are told that, 'He who loses his life for my sake will find it.'

As a counsellor, I can only say that I believe that it is absolutely vital for a child to spend its early years with its own mother. Regular pre-school creches, such as exist throughout Communist Russia, make a mockery of the security of mother-love which every child needs and has a right to. And sadly, it is only later in life that the insecurities and lack of self-worth, engendered by this kind of deprivation, begin to emerge.

When one person is brought in as a kind of nanny, or mother-figure, to help care for the children of a full-time career woman, a different kind of deprivation shows itself—but this time on the part of the mother. A mother-figure who is lovingly and caringly around all the time in the lives of the children inevitably remains a mother-figure, to whom the children will turn in preference to the real thing. Many adults, who were themselves brought up by nannies, still today have a much closer bonding with them than they do with their natural mothers. It is really not possible in this respect to have your cake and eat it!

Two fears usually enter the career-girl's mind at this point. Firstly, how much ground and experience she will lose by going away from her work for so many years, and secondly how on earth she will cope with babies' nappies and only child chatter for what can seem like an eternity!

It may be possible for the career-girl to take on some sort of part-time work—for example, women doctors may run a couple of clinics a week or secretaries may operate a rota with others in a similar position. If this can be done, it is obviously the ideal situation, keeping the mother from the wasteland of boredom and the fear of a mind going to seed, but not depriving the children of her love and attention.

However, more often than not, this really cannot be achieved and the skills we need for our jobs have to go into cold storage at least until the children are of school age.

I myself only overcame the problems of this time of

life by asking God to show me what He wanted me to do with my time. For example, as a housebound young mother I looked at the problems of loneliness experienced by other mums. This led me to start a coffee group in the area, which, incidentally, continues to this day. I also learnt a great deal about the local church, which eventually resulted in my editing the parish magazine, specifically designed for outreach, which was sent to every house in the area. More important still, as I experienced my own inadequacy as a mother (having had a fairly traumatic childhood myself) I started on a Christian counselling course, which completely transformed my experience of life and relationships both inside and outside the family, and from which I have never looked back.

Those nine years of my life, which I thought would be a dull back-water, have I believe given me a much greater wealth of experience with which to return to the world of work—and in addition I have been able to spend that time building a really good relationship with my own children.

Getting our attitudes right

It would be quite wrong to give the impression that a chauvinistic approach to women is the norm in Christian circles today. I have usually found real acceptance and the freedom to put across the feminine viewpoint. But as the anti-feminist drive has got under way in certain Christian circles, some women are beginning to feel more and more unsure of themselves. Many have no particular desire to go along with the feminists, but neither do they see wholesale submission to their husbands as the answer either.

They need to feel loved and valued for themselves, whatever they are doing.

Single women, who already have a considerable burden to bear because of their alone-ness, are also confused about the way forward. The more God uses them in their careers, the more some people in the church seem to frown on their success. What are they to do?

The danger is that other people's opinions may block out anything that God Himself is saying to us. Instead of God's guidance we hear other people's thoughts and there are always enough insecure and uncertain people around to think something unhelpful! If we are to be of any use to God in the world we have first of all to accept ourselves as we are and not struggle ineffectually to be something different.

We live in a lonely, broken world which has for the most part lost sight of God and of anyone who cares. A woman's natural loving gifts can be used in any situation. We must learn to look away from our safe little boxes and our own self-interest and seek ways in which we can help outsiders and show God's love in the world around us. The world needs to see that we care and that we care with no strings attached. While we are sitting around feeling insecure and wondering what our role in society should be, a whole world of people needs our love and our friendship.

We need to catch a vision for our own homes and families. Do our husbands know how much they matter to us or our children how much we value having them around? Very probably we find communication difficult but we must try to listen to what they are feeling and to what their real needs are and not just to talk at them with 'oughts' and 'shoulds'. Are our homes places where they and others feel wanted and where they can be themselves, or are we imposing unnecessary rules, and a self-conscious Christian life-style that drives people away from our doors?

Finally, we need to listen to what God is saying to us concerning His will for our lives. Just as with Deborah, Esther and Ruth in the Old Testament and Mary the mother of Jesus, God has often used women as a part of His world plan. We must be ready to hear what he is saying to us. There are so many areas in which our love and commonsense are needed and, after all, surely the parable of the talents was written for women as well as for men....

Marriage in the Balance

---

by Ann Warren

'But I thought we were so happy . . .'

Marriages are breaking up. Some start off okay, others go downhill right away—and Christian marriages appear to be no exception.

This book takes an essentially practical look at marriage and its Christian foundations. It asks: how can we make it work? If our marriage is on the rocks, what can we do to repair the damage? Or if it's healthy, how do we make it even better?

More specific questions are also tackled, like

How submissive should a wife be?
    and
What priority should Mum and Dad give to the children?

Ann Warren is a freelance journalist and works as a pastoral counsellor. She is married with three children.

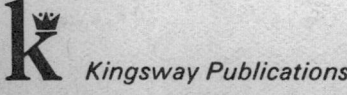

Kingsway Publications